Global Praise for

*All proceeds from the sale of this book
directly support the work of URI.
Thank you.*

A Bishop's Quest:
Founding a United Religions

Cover design, book design by Jerry Kelly, Jenaye Hill
Printed by Printing Arts Press, Mount Vernon, OH

XOXOX

P R E S S

Published by XOXOXpress
102 Gaskin Ave., Box 51, Gambier OH 43022
xoxoxpress.com

Distributed by United Religions Initiative
1009 General Kennedy Ave., San Francisco, CA 94129
uri.org

Library of Congress Cataloging-in-Publication Data

Swing, William E., 1936-
  A bishop's quest : founding a united religions / the Right Reverend
William E. Swing, Episcopal Bishop of California (retired). -- First
[edition].
      pages cm
  ISBN 978-1-880977-38-5
  1. Swing, William E., 1936- 2. Episcopal Church 3. Episcopal
Church--California--Bishops--Biography. 4. Religions (Proposed,
universal, etc.) 5. United Religions Initiative. I. Title.
  BX5995.S955A3 2015
  201'.5--dc23
                                    2014040822

A Bishop's Quest:
Founding a United Religions

The Right Reverend
William E. Swing
Episcopal Bishop of California, VII

XOXOX
PRESS

Contents

Acknowledgements

I want to thank Mary Swing for the journey. I want to honor William and Ute Bowes, who believed in me from the beginning and backed me strongly every step of the way. At the start and for many years along the way, Ann and Archibald McClure and Richard Goldman provided funds that helped keep URI afloat and moving forward. Thanks, too, for all of the firsts: Charles Gibbs, the First Executive Director, Rita Semel, the first Global Council Chair, and John Weiser, the first Chair of the President's Council. I salute Rupert and Maryellie Johnson for helping to move URI to a higher dimension. I appreciate the brilliant work of Sally Mahé who has been serving every day of URI's life and just keeps on going. I thank Sandra Gary for acting as my writing coach for this book.

Introduction

The first Episcopal bishop in the United States was consecrated in 1789. Seven hundred and thirty-two bishops later, in 1979, I was consecrated. Actually, the line of bishops who had hands laid on their heads by at least three other bishops of the historic line goes back almost two thousand years. For the purposes of this book, I only want to make the undisputed point that my number in line in the Episcopal Church of the United States of America is 732.

In February 1993, I stepped out of line. Well, not exactly out of line, but with one foot firmly on the line of bishops, I placed my other foot on the line of an initiative to create a United Religions. My feet were parallel, and I began skiing forward for thirteen years at a fast pace, and covered hundreds of thousands of miles on an extraordinary journey. On one ski I was bishop number 732. On the other ski I was number one, the Founder of the United Religions Initiative. How did that come about?

In an intense moment of introspection in February, 1993 I was overwhelmed by a series of haunting and scandalous questions:

If the *nations* of the world have met through representatives every day for fifty years to struggle together for global good, why have the *religions* of the world not met together at least once for the same purpose?

With the ascendancy of militant religious fundamentalists, why haven't the religions joined together to address and strategize around violent ethnic and tribal agendas of religions?

Since doctors, lawyers, scholars, scientists and others have come together to hold each other accountable, why have religions totally avoided mutual accountability?

Is there no neutral place on earth for someone to bring a grievance about the misuse of religion?

Since the zeal for conversions lends itself to gross exploitation, have the religions of the world ever sat down to discuss the usefulness and harm of missionary activities?

If the key evangelical strategy of major religions, growing new members, is to have as many babies as possible, does there ever come a moral moment or discussion among religions about over-population, limited environmental resources and sustainability of life on this planet?

Do religions think that the present status of equilibrium among religions is the best that it could possibly be and therefore pleasing to God, or is there a quiet shame about the irresponsible behavior of faiths in relation to each other?

Are religions ready to exist in context of an emerging global civilization or content to operate in cultural and tribal ghettoes? Do religions exist to conquer the world or to serve the world?

In 1993 I thought that the best way to answer these questions and to do something positive was to go on a quest. I would pursue the creation of a United Religions. Although I had no idea of what a United Religions would be or would do, I figured that if I leapt into the arena of faiths deeply enough, proclaiming the coming of a United Religions, the answer could be discovered. This book is the story of my quest: the quest of bishop 732 trying to be of service in bridging religion's divide!

Chapter 1
The Night of My Fifth Vow

On a dreary day in February 1993, I was in my office at Diocesan House at Grace Cathedral atop San Francisco's Nob Hill, sitting at a desk that had survived two major earthquakes. The phone rang. On the other end was Gillian Sorenson, the United Nations Assistant Secretary for External Relations. I sat up straighter as I heard her tell me that a big anniversary was coming up. The United Nations was going to turn fifty years old in two years, and the Secretary General wanted to come back to San Francisco where the U.N. Charter had been written and signed.

"Would you host a large celebratory event at Grace Cathedral?" she asked. "I would be honored to do that," I said. Gillian told me she envisioned all of the nations and all of the religions of the world gathered together in the Cathedral for that commemoration service. She said that the United Nations would bring 185 ambassadors of the world. And then came the life-changing question for me. "Would you bring representatives of all of the religions of the world?" I was so stunned by the question that I deadpanned, "I'm not doing anything much this afternoon and I'll make a few phone calls." My silly response was merely an effort to buy time as the profundity of her request began to work its way into my brain.

All of the religions in the world? Racing through my mind were lots of questions. How many religions were there in the world— major religions, minority religions, religions recognized by their governments, indigenous traditions and tribes? I soon found out that the Internal Revenue Service of the U.S. recognized 258 religions and granted them tax privileges. Who were the religious leaders? How would I set criteria for deciding who would make the cut and who would be excluded? For instance, how many Christian Protestant denominations are there? And how many of them are breakaway groups? How many enemies can I make by inviting some and not others? And who in the world am I to decide? Gillian had asked a terrible question and I felt I wanted to backpedal as fast as I could to get my bearings. Nevertheless, at the same time, I wanted to be a good host. So I reluctantly agreed to bring together representatives of all of the religions of the world.

When I went to bed that night, I felt weighted down and my head was swirling. All of the religions of the world! All nations of the world had forged a common vocation for the good of the world through the creation of the United Nations. For fifty years they had met daily. On the other hand, during the same fifty years, the religions had never come together for one day to exercise a common vocation for the good of the world. The world's religions have no heart or no courage to serve the world together. In my mind it seemed that what was needed was a United Religions to provide religions with a place to gather, to hold each other accountable, and from which to take joint actions for the world's sake.

An awful door in my mind came ajar on that night and the full weight of what I glimpsed on the other side of the door landed on my conscience. Something in religion was terribly wrong. It wasn't the behaviors that I had witnessed in San Francisco in my years of episcopacy, everything from naughty to felonious to vicious. It was deeper than those predictable human frailties. The problem was primitive and structural. Religion cannot abide religions. A religion does not know what to do with other religions operating nearby.

Or more to the point, religion knows what to do: namely destroy the other religions so that there would only be one religion. It stands to reason that if there is only One God, then there must only be one religion to respond to that One God. Everything else in the realm of religion is a threat, a distortion, a usurper. Religions therefore must be destroyed by religion. And if that is not possible, then religions must be conquered and subjugated. And if that is not possible, religions must be coerced and intimidated. And if that is not possible they must be tolerated. At best! Isn't there something beyond reluctant religious toleration?

What I glimpsed in that door ajar were the countless millions of religious people who have been raped, tortured, imprisoned, brutally murdered in Name of the God of religion. Although their cry has an echo, the logic behind their demise was unchallenged. Their mounting suffering was not subsiding at the end of the 20th century; it was increasing. And it is never just one religion against another. It is also the competition for authenticity within a religion. Who is a "real" Christian and not a fraud? Who "truly is a Jew" and not a fake? Who is "a genuine Muslim" and not a heretic? The answer to those questions is often pursued with a bomb or a bullet, or if those means are thwarted, then through the toxic stagnation of religious tribalism.

For a second, but only for a second, I allowed myself to consider the first of the Ten Commandments. Primitive and structural! "Thou shalt have none other gods but me." If a religion prides itself on keeping the first of the Ten Commandments, then it will pride itself on what it does about the "other gods." Holy writings will be filled with the stories of how the people of the other gods were slain, and the purity of the religion was maintained against the threat of assimilation. How can history compete with the Divine command to have "none other gods"? If the planet Earth is ever going to have a chance of continuing as a cosmic oasis in the vastness of the universe, perhaps we need to take a second look at the first Commandment.

I was drifting toward a new vow and a new basic covenant between myself and the God of all mercies—in addition to the vows I had made as a husband, a deacon, a priest, and a bishop. On that night in February 1993, I made up my mind that I could do an adequate, if imperfect, job in getting together representatives of all of the world's religions for a one-hour celebration of the U.N.'s 50th Anniversary. After all, no one expects much from religions coming together. Almost any assemblage of representatives would be acceptable to the U.N.

But lurking behind the assignment was the riveting burden of attempting something profound on the world stage: finding a way for people of all faiths to keep their faiths and at the same time realize a common vocation for the sake of the world. I was ready to commit to be a catalyst for the creation of a United Religions. I, who had never taken a course in comparative religions, I, who knew little about others religions and had not cared to learn more, I was ready to take my fifth vow. And the bewildering thing was that I had no idea, no idea whatsoever, what a United Religions would look like or how it should be developed. The best that I could imagine was that a United Religions would somehow parallel the United Nations but in ways and forms that would be appropriate for the various religions.

It felt like God was shoving me onto a large stage, and I didn't know my lines. Lots of people were going to stare at me now as they listened to my February vision and vow. I could easily anticipate the skepticism that awaited me. On the one hand, I told myself, I only signed on to be a catalyst for the creation of a United Religions. After all, no one in the world was expecting me to take a step in an interfaith direction, let alone a bold step. I could simply raise the prospect, then step aside at the appropriate moment and let another person or another generation drive the idea forward. Hadn't President Woodrow Wilson pushed for the League of Nations in the early part of the 20th century? But it wasn't until the end of World War II that his general thinking came to maturity in the United Nations. On the other hand, what if my vision took on a life of its own and I would be strapped to it for the rest of my life?

I knew how vows worked. You sign an inward, invisible covenant with God and work at it for all your days, good and bad, with successes and failures, days in the wilderness and moments of breakthroughs. In February 1993, I made my fifth vow.

Chapter 2
Searching for Colleagues

Every bishop has a chair. It is called a "cathedra." And wherever the bishop's chair is located, the cathedral of that bishop's diocese is also located. In 1993 my "cathedra" was situated in Grace Cathedral, San Francisco. The priest in charge of a cathedral on behalf of the bishop is called a Dean, and the dean's job is to run the day-to-day operations. In my case, the Dean of Grace Cathedral was the Very Rev. Alan Jones. Bishops and Deans get very touchy about who, exactly, is in charge of a cathedral at great moments. Each can make a claim.

So when I volunteered to the U.N. that Grace Cathedral would host the big U.N. 50th Anniversary celebration, I immediately ran next door from to my office on Nob Hill to the cathedral, and inquired if Dean Alan Jones was up to the task. He was, with reservations. First of all, he expected to be entirely in charge of the U.N. 50th Celebration in the cathedral. Clearly, local representatives from various faith traditions would have to have a voice in the planning, but as long as he was ultimately the boss, he would be my colleague in this monumental adventure.

Second, he insisted on knowing if the massive construction project—costing $22.4 million to complete the "close" (campus) of Grace Cathedral—would be finished by the time of the June 26, 1995, U.N. 50th celebration. Although I could not guarantee a precise date of completion for the project we were leading together, I was aware that the contractors had predicted a finish well before June 26, 1995. So I assured him it would be finished, although both of us realized that the timing might be problematic. We were risking it together.

And third, when I told him about my vision of a United Religions, and using this occasion to launch the idea in the world, he was totally uninterested and dismissive. He wanted nothing to do with it. Fair enough! I was on my own.

When he asked me for specifics about a United Religions, I had almost nothing to say. As dumb as it sounds, I figured that if I simply held up two words, "United Religions," people with far greater knowledge of religious dialogues and interfaith experiences could take it from there and imagine their way to a new reality. My job would be simply to initiate the conversation. How's that for stupid naiveté? This was akin to assuming that a pipefitter or a registered nurse could merely come up with a couple of letters, and pronounce that E=MC squared, and then wait for mathematicians and physicists to figure out what the formula meant. I could make an argument about why it would be a good idea to have a United Religions, but I couldn't paint a picture of how it would operate. Dean Alan Jones was merely the first person to discover how shallow my thinking was. I actually knew that before he did. But it didn't stop me.

So I had a colleague for the U.N. 50th celebration, but not for a United Religions.

Next, I went looking for colleagues in the world of international interfaith work. Again, I had no knowledge. I figured that there must be inspired people around the world bringing people of various religions together and doing noble work. Maybe they were yearning for a United Religions. I could learn from them. And perhaps recruit them. This began an education process for me. I discovered that the largest group was the World Conference on Religions for Peace (WCRP), which dealt with the great religious leaders of the world. Dr. William Vendley was their Secretary General. Then there was the International Association for Religious Freedom (IARF) headed by Dr. Robert Traer. The list I compiled went on and on. I telephoned each and every one of them and invited them to meet me at the U.N. in New York on June 13, 1993 to explore what role they could play in the big U.N. 50th celebration in 1995 and explore other matters as well, such as the coming United Religions.

To their enormous credit, they all showed up, including the Rev. Marcus Braybrooke of the Congress of Faiths, Father Lois Dolan of the Temple of Understanding, and Daniel Gomez Ibanez of the Parliament of World Religions (which was to have its second meeting in one hundred years coincidentally with my invitation). Although we had an exciting freewheeling discussion, it was abundantly clear that none of them wanted anything to do with the creation of a United Religions. It seemed like an alien idea to them. Too far-fetched! Too bureaucratic! Too much money required! Too threatening to religions and to international interfaith organizations! I invited them to be on hand at the U.N. 50th celebrations, and several accepted the invitation.

Although I made some life-long friends that day as well as some life-long antagonists, I had no colleagues for a United Religions. The one little glimmer of hope came from Marcus Braybrooke, who hailed from Oxford, England. He suggested that if ever there would be a United Religions, it would most likely come from young people. So just before the June 26, 1995, event, he suggested that I hold a youth event. I leapt at that one piece of positive advice.

What started out as a U.N. 50th Anniversary celebration, quickly took on two additional challenges, a Youth Conference and the launching of the idea for the creation of a United Religions. I needed lots of help and right away. Two Episcopal priests from the Diocese of California came forward to help me out, The Rev. William Nern and the Rev. Charles Gibbs. So the number of colleagues I sought was growing, by a small fraction.

Finding people to plan the one-hour celebration service at Grace Cathedral was relatively easy. The San Francisco interfaith leaders knew each other well and were eager to put in the two years of planning for the U.N. 50th Celebration on June 26, 1995. A close friend and strong interfaith leader, Rita Semel, had everyone's confidence, so she and I convened an ongoing planning group along with Dean Alan Jones.

Finding people to plan and execute the Youth Conference proved more difficult. The group planning the U.N. 50th service also became tasked with planning the Youth Conference. But that group had to find a campus on which to hold the event and a faculty to work with the students on the subject of The Coming United Religions. Fortunately we came upon the University of San Francisco and ended up renting their space and employing a few of their faculty to work on the Coming United Religions.

One of the main reasons for the University's readiness to host our group on their campus was that we had enlisted quite an illustrious list of speakers: South African Archbishop Desmond Tutu; Pakistani Supreme Court Justice Javid Iqbal; leader of Reformed Judaism Rabbi Alfred Gottschalk; Harvard Professor of Religion Diana Eck; influential Rabbi David Saperstein; Nobel Prize winner Betty Williams; and Black

Muslim leader W. Dean Mohammed. So I was beginning to gather a number of substantial people for both the Youth Conference and the U.N. 50th. As for a United Religions, I was almost completely on my own.

Actually the youth event didn't work out the way I had envisioned. Yes, I did recruit 200 young people, raised almost all of the $278,000 required, and had stellar group of speakers. But then, to my horror, at the last minute, the University of San Francisco faculty changed the direction of the youth conference. They wanted it to have nothing to do with the idea of a United Religions. They ordered me not to mention a United Religions in my letter of welcome to the students, threatening to revoke our agreement if I did. They changed the youth conference to be about "Rediscovering Justice," a subject familiar to them. I assumed that they were not keen on teaching about a United Religions that did not exist, and couldn't figure out a curriculum for such a short course. On the other hand, they regularly taught classes on rediscovering justice and this was in their comfort zone.

This put the entire conference in jeopardy. The students and the illustrious speakers would be arriving in two weeks, and I was on the brink of being kicked off the University campus or just walking away. But to where? It was too late to move to another campus. After some heated words, they "allowed" me to mention the words "United Religions" in my opening letter of welcome but they insisted on teaching courses only about Rediscovering Justice. Personally, I faced the herculean task of not letting my anger at that faculty dominate all that was about to happen. Interestingly, ten years later, I was given an honorary doctorate degree in Humane Letters from the University of San Francisco and delivered the Baccalaureate address at graduation. So we became friends, and I became a grateful alumnus.

When the students arrived, I greeted them with these words, which riled the faculty:

"You have entered into the genesis of a vision when you signed on for this conference. As I mentioned in my letter to you, a vision came first before the conference and actually caused this conference to happen. This is the vision: We are going to dare to challenge the world of religions to make a great change. Heretofore when wars threatened, when the environment was despoiled, when human rights were violated, the great religions of the world did not convene to speak of these atrocities or to raise their voices together to say or to do anything. We intend for this conference to speak to the world and call for the creation of something entirely new. Just as there has been a United Nations in New York for the past fifty years, we are going to the cathedral on Sunday and will call for the creation of a parallel organization, the United Religions, to meet on a regular basis to address issues of global good and call for accountability among the religious traditions. This is the vision that will intertwine this conference.

"What would a United Religions look like, specifically? We have had folks working on an answer to that question for the past few years. A third draft of an 'Initiative for the United Religions Organization' is on your chairs tonight and is the product of that work. It is not intended to be tablets carved in stone coming down from on high but a working document for our future, to be of use in perfecting an even more detailed description of what the vision calls for."

A strong element of schizophrenia was inlaid into the Youth Conference. The faculty taught in their comfort zone of justice. I took every informal and formal opportunity to splice in thoughts about a coming United Religions. As for the youth, they picked up the competing themes, and half way through the conference, they staged a protest pleading for the leaders to declare what this conference was basically about. This was never resolved. When the students were taught, the theme was Rediscovering Justice. When the religious leaders had discussion early in the morning or late in the afternoon or evening, the topic was always about the United Religions Organization.

I asked a Bay Area activist, Peter Hart, to create a white paper that would take the organizational design of the United Nations and impose it on the religions of the world to see what conversations and insights it would evoke. Actually, it was quite clear why a United Religions could never parallel the United Nations. The challenge of representation or "representativity" could never be overcome. We all realized what a United Religions would not look like. But what a proper United Religions might look like was never glimpsed—although not for lack of trying. At the end of the Youth Conference I did not come away with any colleagues from the religious leaders, the interfaith leaders, the students, and certainly not from the faculty of the University of San Francisco. All I had was a couple of people who had planned the conference and the celebration.

One unexpected person, Richard Blum, did step forward. Although he was passionate about starting his own interfaith organization called "The Foundation for Religious Understanding," Richard, who is the husband of Senator Dianne Feinstein, rolled up his sleeves to help me. And since he was a close friend of His Holiness, the Dalai Lama, Richard made sure that Lodi Gyari, Special Envoy of the Dalai Lama, participated in our conference. In the back of my mind, I figured that if I could get two of the most self-evident spiritual leaders in the world, the Dalai Lama and Archbishop Desmond Tutu, to back the coming United Religions, I would have a large boost in realizing the vision. Richard made the introduction to one of the two people I was seeking.

Lodi Gyari, after lots of questions and probably off-scene conversations with the Dalai Lama, expressed an interest in the topic of a United Religions. But the only way for me to take it from there was to make a trip to India and speak with His Holiness in Dharamsala. Lodi invited me, and I planned to make that journey within the year.

Desmond Tutu, on the other hand, was there on campus, so this crucial conversation was readily available. Previously, I had managed some of his itinerary for speeches in California. We became friends, and eventually he invited me to his enthronement as Archbishop of South Africa, and I did attend. But when it came to participating in this Youth Conference, he didn't want to do it. And how could I blame him for that? In the week before our conference he had to fly from South Africa to Taiwan and back—twice. Yet I begged for his help. Also, he wanted to stay home in South Africa that week and watch his country's rugby team play for the World Cup championship. I promised that if he came, I would get the owner of an Irish pub to open up at 5:00 a.m. so that Desmond could sit at the bar with a cup of coffee and watch South Africa triumph. To my utmost joy, he agreed to attend.

Enlisting his full support in the creation of a United Religions was another matter. First I told him about my idea of the

United Religions and having him and the Dalai Lama as its "Champions." With their endorsement and leadership, we could begin to attract other religious leaders who could develop a charter and organizational design for the coming United Religions. Although I was talking about religious leaders creating their own United Religions, he was hearing something else. He thought that I was trying to create another international interfaith movement—which I certainly did not intend to do. Desmond Tutu said that he already worked with the interfaith group World Conference of Religions for Peace, which zeroes in on religious leaders. He said that he also worked with the Parliament of World Religions, which just held a spectacular world gathering of faith traditions in Chicago in 1993. He didn't want to get involved with me because he thought that I was trying to create an international interfaith group that would compete with already existing and successful organizations. This conversation was devastating for me. I was hoping to gain a colleague in Desmond Tutu, but for all of his thoughtfulness to me, he simply could not do that. His rejection was crushing. But I couldn't merely stop. A Youth Conference was going on. The U.N. 50th was fast approaching. And I was trying to launch a vision for a coming United Religions.

Unbeknownst to me, the clue to my interfaith future lay in a group of people that, at the time, seemed the least likely. The youth! What a crowd! They were quick to protest. In less than 24 hours they walked out of a talk by former Congressman Pete McCloskey saying that they were sick and tired of not having all of their needs met, including such needs as dietary, psychological, and religious, and they refused to come back until the planners got it right. Here were 200 young people from 68 religions and they insisted on immediate perfection from us in meeting their every need. We provided them with some of the most important religious voices of the world to be available to them for formal talks and informal conversations. We raised almost a third of a million dollars so that they had to pay nothing. In the long run, in my recollection, not one of them ever had anything to do with the United Religions Initiative.

But, as a group they carried the seed of the future vision of a United Religions. It happened all at once. And as expected, in a walkout protest of sorts. In the middle of a lengthy plenary session, one young person after another got up and walked across the street and onto a big lawn. When a large enough group arrived, they held hands and prayed and sang songs of their traditions—Muslims, Jews, Christians, Buddhists, Hindus, and on and on. Before our very eyes we witnessed a grass-roots display of spontaneity, all around good-heartedness, and an amateur sense of belonging together. I couldn't help but think at the time that in getting ready for the U.N. 50th service at Grace Cathedral, it took over a dozen people working for two years to design a liturgy that would not be offensive to some traditions, and here were these young people making it up as they went along in a matter of minutes.

That was it. That was the United Religions which I was looking for but didn't have the prescience to notice. What I was looking for was something that would take place in a cathedral, not in a large field. While various religions were jockeying to be heard, while interfaith leaders were posturing for precedence, while China was sweating the arrival of the Dalai Lama, under the radar an interfaith service broke out. Natural, spontaneous, filled with a sense of the moment! It suggested that what the world needed now was not a bureaucratically layered, antiseptically sanctioned rule of engagement, but rather the good-hearted participation of people of all faiths.

Years later, this pivot to interfaith expression broke out in the U.S. following a series of bloody killings on college campuses, at major community events, at religious institutions, and in schools. Let me ask a question: What do the following tragedies have in common? The Columbine High School shooting of April 1999; the Virginia Tech University mass killings of April 2007; the Boston Marathon bombing of April 2013; and the Jewish Community Center murders of April 2104? And the answer isn't "April."

In all of those situations, an interfaith worship service followed immediately. People of all faiths realized in an instant that they share the same grief and that they need to draw strength from each other. There were no theological papers written, no protocols distributed about how feelings should be expressed liturgically. Interfaith services sprang up, and centuries of suspicions were discarded instantly as people looked around and recognized that in a profound way, their destinies were linked together.

What the world needed now was not one organization anchored in one city but tens of thousands of a little United Religions on a scale that everyone in the world, in every locale in the world, had access to. In the little United Religions, a world of differing believers could grieve together, celebrate together, and change their communities for the better together. But in 1996, I just didn't notice.

The end of the conference was like a Fellini movie, where a motorcycle barrels through the scene for no apparent reason. For us, it was a well-dressed Japanese businessman showing up with no invitation or credentials. He sat down, listened for a while, never spoke, and quietly left. He was either a man from the moon or from Rev. Moon. Later on, after Desmond

Tutu and Betty Williams gave bell-ringing talks, a man from Marin County, California, jumped up with Hawaiian leis and ten Hawaiians to sing ethnic spiritual songs. A Youth Conference like no other! I failed in finding colleagues, but my vision got its first test.

Chapter 3
The 50th Anniversary of the United Nations

The morning of June 25, 1995 dawned hot, and would soon reach 100 degrees. As I worked on my few lines and toured Grace Cathedral's newly-finished construction, the youth from the conference were gearing up for a march from the university to the cathedral. At the same time, Princess Margaret of England was deciding whether or not to walk up our newly-minted stairway in front of Grace Cathedral. Lech Walesa of Poland was falling into place between his bodyguards. The Chinese were searching intently to see if the Dalai Lama would actually show up. The musicians were tuning up. Waters from Lourdes and the Ganges and other sacred sources around the world were being poured into Grace Cathedral's Fountain of San Francisco, this first water for the new fountain. The San Francisco dignitaries and the United Nations leaders formed a receiving line. And Mary and I stood just inside the magnificent Ghiberti doors of the Cathedral to welcome our illustrious guests. It was glorious. But not all went smoothly.

During the prelude, the Sikhs sang too long. The Jewish choir sang too long. The pre-event was falling farther and farther behind, just as it was time for the television coverage. We could delay no longer. So the Secretary General of the United Nations Boutros-Boutros Ghali was greeted, and the British Royal Philharmonic began.

Someone on the roof of the cathedral tripped and knocked over the critical television transmitter. Thus, no coverage! But far worse, the Native Americans who had planned to call in the Spirits of the North, South, East, and West had to be scratched because the others had gone over their time limits. These folks had prepared for two years for the moment that never came. The pain that came from that hard decision had to be carried by master of ceremonies, the Rev. Susan Singer.

My insides were tightly wound. Here was the moment when I was going to announce to the world the coming of a United Religions. The Dean of Grace Cathedral thought it was a frivolous idea. The faculty of the University of San Francisco thought it was unmentionable. Desmond Tutu wouldn't touch it. At least the young man chosen by the Youth Conference to preach could preach about the coming United Religions. But after being tutored by a university professor, he actually preached on Rediscovering Justice, of all subjects. I could feel my humanity and vigor slipping away. Nevertheless, with the little time I had, I still talked about what religions could do in response to the 50 years of the U.N.'s life—that the religions could create a United Religions. I got the words out.

A woman sang a song in the Farsi language, and somehow it touched a deep place for most everyone seated there. All of a sudden, the nervousness permeating the grand cathedral space lifted, and everything that followed was applauded or appreciated or brilliantly received. The United Nations could not have had a more special moment. At the end, I invited everyone to hold hands with the persons next to them for the final silence and blessing for nations and religions. Afterwards I discovered that "royals" did not hold hands in such settings. But it was a lesson learned in good humor.

While the notables retired to the Chapel of Grace for pictures, our daughter, Alice, who is short, said that seeing short Tutu, short Princess Margaret, and short Lech Walesa, she will never again look up to world leaders. Nevertheless, she and everyone else were overwhelmed by what had just happened. All of the nations and all of the religions in one place at one time celebrating a conspicuous hope for the world being realized in a United Nations for half of a century! All were feeling ennobled by what had just taken place.

The Korean Wan Buddhist representative to the U.N. Religious NGO group, The Ven. Chung Ok Lee, followed me to my office and described an interesting scene. She said that the United Nations was one wheel of a cart that was moving awkwardly. What was needed was a second wheel, the one of spirituality and religion, a United Religions. With two wheels, the cart can do the job properly. I filed that thought away.

U.N. 50th events kept right on coming. First, a dinner with Nobel Laureates! Some of them spoke positively about the need for a United Religions. I sat next to Shridath (Sonny) Ramphal, an Indian who grew up in the Caribbean. He predicted that nations in the future will not continue to be nations as we have known them. Peoples' nationalism will still be there but triumphalism and loyalties will give way to a nebulous community that crosses all of the borders. Multinational corporations have already learned to profit from this, and someday the idea of multi-religions operating under an interfaith umbrella will be thinkable. Again, I filed that thought for the future.

Even on the next day, June 27, an impressive event took place at the beautifully decorated War Memorial Opera House in San Francisco. The United States' Ambassador to the U.N. Madeline Albright spoke powerfully, as did President Bill Clinton. Then we went to the Moscone Center for the Grand Finale honoring U.N. General Secretary Boutros Boutros-

Ghali. In an outstanding speech, he asked all of us to imagine a world without a United Nations. All I could manage to do was to imagine a world without a United Religions, and it looked exactly like the world that exists.

Making the very last event was the hardest. On Tuesday, July 28, Mary and I were supposed to be at the home of the Japanese Consul General for a dinner honoring the Chief of Protocol for the city of San Francisco, Richard Goldman. My problem was that I had to wake up very early and fly to Indianapolis, Indiana, to see if I could get enough money from the Eli Lilly Foundation to pay the last bills of the Youth Conference. Getting back to San Francisco in time was the challenge. I struck out completely with Lilly, got on a plane, and made it back just in time. Mary sat at dinner with the all-time great baseball star, Willie Mays, and that proved to be a fitting wrap-up to the U.N. 50th celebration.

Chapter 4
The Morning After the Night Before

Friday morning at 9:00 a.m., June 30, 1995, was a signal moment in the unfolding life of the United Religions Initiative. It was a make or break time. Sitting in my living room were six people who had worked hard to bring off the major events of the Youth Conference and the U.N. 50th Celebration: David Ponedel, a cook from Berkeley, California, who would soon be back to cooking; Rabbi David Davis, who would soon leave town to assume another position; Peter Hart, who would soon be out of the life of the initiative for a United Regions; the Rev. William Nern, who would resume his duties in housing 800 homeless people on a nightly basis; Rita Semel, who had asked me three days before where we were going next, and said, "We can't stop now!"; and the Rev. Charles Gibbs, who was going back to be the Rector of Incarnation Episcopal Church in San Francisco! Although we were giddy with success and exchanged hugs and high-fives, nevertheless there was a mood in the air that felt like Cinderella just after the clock struck midnight.

As dopey as it may seem, the seven of us were sitting there debating how we were going to change the course of human history. I thought, "You've got to be kidding! The seven of us?" It was an insane conversation. The context had completely changed. No longer was there a mandate from the United Nations. No longer were there famous people rushing in. No longer was there an agenda that would warrant raising money. All that existed of the United Religions was the seven of us. So what did we have going for us?

We had a stack of calling cards from diplomats around the world. Lodi Gyari had promised me a meeting with the Dalai

Lama in India. The Ven. Chung Ok Lee had invited me to address the religious NGOs at the United Nations in October. And a couple of San Francisco newspaper articles had praised the idea of a United Religions headquartered in San Francisco. It wasn't much, but it was a start.

With some of the people who had worked on the recent big events, we volunteered to create a "Host Committee" that would address the ongoing concerns of the United Religions. In time, newer people would join. It would be a loose group with a standing invitation for anyone off the street to join in, and literally, people came in off the street. Since I had advertised that in exactly one year, June 26, 1997, there would be a follow-up conference in San Francisco whose agenda would be to plan for the writing of the charter of the United Religions, this Host Group would have a serious task. I chaired the group, and its life would become chaotic and lovely and actually accomplish its ambitious tasks.

About this time it became clear that the Rev. Charles Gibbs was stepping up his commitment. First, he volunteered to accompany me when I spoke at the U.N. in October. Then he arranged to take a sabbatical from his parish in order to provide leadership for the First United Religions Summit in 1996, to be held at the Fairmont Hotel.

As for me, I had many factors to consider if I were to go forward. What about the Diocese of California? I could only guess at how much time it would take to create a United Religions. Should I back out now, and content myself with having raised the prospect of a United Religions in a conspicuous setting? Should I give all of my time back to the Diocese of California? Could I continue to live two lives and two vocations at the same time?

The elephant in the room was the question of how I would take the next step—travel around the world and arrange appointments with the world's most important religious leaders. Why in the world would they want to talk with me? And whatever would persuade them that a United Religions was desirable or doable? When they asked me what a United Religions would look like, and what exactly it would do, and who would be involved, I knew that I would have no cogent answer for them. I would be selling a process that would lead to a new creation, but wasn't the creation itself. Could I pull that off? Perhaps I could get William Levada, then the Roman Catholic Archbishop of San Francisco, to get me an appointment at the Vatican. Might my Greek Orthodox friend, George Marcus, be able to get me an appointment with the Ecumenical Patriarch in Istanbul? Certainly, as an Anglican bishop, I could get an appointment with the Archbishop of Canterbury. Or, could I? Perhaps not. Merely getting the appointments would be major undertakings for me.

Where would I find the time to make such journeys? The principle answer was that I could take a sabbatical, something I had done only once, for three months, in my sixteen years as bishop. Since I had no assisting bishop to help with the diocese, and since I had not missed one day of work due to illness in those 16 years, the parishioners around the Bay Area were accustomed to seeing me on duty each day. Taking a sabbatical of three months would be new behavior for me and for them. So I would have to make thorough plans for the diocese to be covered if I took an absence of three months in the spring of 1996.

Then arose the question of how to pay for such a journey, and whether or not I could raise enough money so that Mary could make the journey also. No one answer was possible. I would have to cobble together monies from multiple sources. Someone suggested that I try the Gerbode Foundation in San Francisco. A friend in Washington, D.C., suggested that I try with the newly formed Christopher Columbus Foundation. For years I had been invited to be a preacher at the Mar Thoma Convention in India, a convention that would pay my and Mary's way to India and back. I could say yes to them and get off to a free start. Of course, the Diocese of California had a fund to assist me on a sabbatical. Then I could try to find places that we could stay for no rent or for very little, trusting in the kindness of strangers. Then too, Mary and I could spend my monthly salary on the road instead of spending it in San Francisco. So, the one critical assignment for me would be to find as much money from as many sources as I could imagine, so that I could meet with religious leaders around the world. I knew that when the time came to take off, I would have most of this problem solved, and would have to go on faith that situations on the journey would make up the shortfall. At worst, I could take out a loan upon my return. In addition, I would have to be the sole fundraiser for the First Summit of the United Religions which would take place upon my return. My work was cut out for me.

The history of the United Religions Initiative will cite Sunday, June 25, 1995, as the day of the big launch. Yes, it was huge. But the big day didn't unfold in that cathedral. The big launch took place in the Swings' living room at 2006 Lyon Street, San Francisco on Friday, June 30, at 9:00a.m., when seven of us who had been working so hard, gathered to debrief on all that had taken place. While looking at our recent past, our future broke out, and we dedicated ourselves to create a United Religions. We, who had feasted sumptuously at the banquet, decided to make a meal of the leftovers. Of course, four of the seven would be gone from the table soon. But three (Gibbs, Semel, and Swing) would prove to be plenty enough to get started on an arduous, unpredictable, and wildly successful adventure.

Chapter 5
What Will the Folks Back Home Think?

On June 30, 1995, I had to think about more people than the
six others in the room. I had to consider all of the people of
the Episcopal Diocese of California. All 45,000 of them had
elected me 16 years ago to advance the mission of the
Church. They had not elected me to start a United Religions.
What would they think when I told them about my commitment of this day? I hadn't been elected to tilt at wind-
mills. Of course the six other people in the room were not
risking anything. I was the one who had a lot of explaining
to do, and a lot was riding on the reactions of other people—lots of other people. Earlier, on October 11, 1993, I said
in my address to the Diocesan Convention, "I have dedicated myself to being a catalyst for the creation of an institution which will, in some ways, be parallel to the United
Nations—the creation of a United Religions. There should
not only be a United Nations in New York but a United Religions in San Francisco, where the great religions of the
world would meet daily to struggle together for global
good." This comment did not spark a large negative reaction, so I kept on going.

Now that the U.N. 50th celebration was over and the cathedral "close" was completed, the people of the diocese probably thought that life would get back to normal. What would
they think when I told them that I was now going to work full
time on the Diocese—and also full time on the creation of a
United Religions? Not knowing the answer to that question,
I traveled around the Diocese for two years preaching, each
Sunday, on Chapter 10 of the Book of Acts. It told the story of
the Apostle Simon Peter, who following a dream, walked into
the home of a Roman Centurion named Cornelius. Simon

Peter looked at this "non-believer," who was obviously a good man, and said, "I do believe that God shows no partiality, but in every nation, anyone who prays to God and does what is right is acceptable." How far could I go as a bishop with the non-partiality of God toward a United Religions? I preached and listened for two years to what the folks "back home" in the diocese of California thought.

This sort of listening, discussing, and asking was not new. As a matter of fact, I started discovering early that entirely new worlds could open to me. For instance, when I was eleven years old in 1947, my father came home from a bar on a Saturday night in May, woke me up and announced that he had two tickets to tomorrow's double-header baseball game between the Brooklyn Dodgers and our beloved Cincinnati Reds. So we awoke early, drove down to Kentucky, crossed the Ohio River and were in our seats at Crosley Field in Cincinnati just in time for batting practice. Crosley Field, on the next night, was going to be the scene of the light-heavyweight championship fight—a fight between the champ Joey Maxim, whom all the boys on 26th Street despised, and the challenger Gus Lesnevich, whom we all adored.

To my utter amazement, Joey Maxim walked down our aisle and sat next to me. To my delirious amazement, Gus Lesnevich walked down our aisle and sat next to Dad. Figuring that I had to say something on such a moment, I turned to the champ and asked, "Mr. Maxim, may I have your autograph?" To which he replied, "Kid, I came here to watch a baseball game, not to sign autographs." It could not have been a better reply, because he said it loudly enough for Gus to hear. At which point, Gus Lesnevich leaned over my Dad and asked me, "Hey, kid, have you ever met the

Brooklyn Dodgers?" When I said no, he got up, took me by the hand, walked past Joey Maxim, and we marched down the stairs to toward the field. He opened the gate and there we were in the middle of batting practice. He turned to me and asked, "Hey, kid, what's your name?" I said, "Billy Swing." He said, "Billy, I'd like you to meet Jackie." I said, "Hello, Mr. Robinson." He said, "Billy, I'd like you to meet Pee Wee." And I said, "Hello, Mr. Reese." And on and on until I had met almost every one of the famous "Boys of Summer." Finally, he shouted at the Brooklyn manager, Burt Shotton, and asked if he would allow me to sit in the dugout and watch the double-header with him. He agreed happily.

Then came Monday, the day of the big fight, and all of the boys were gathered on 26th Street talking about how we yearned for Gus to win. Then one of the boys turned to me and asked, "Billy, we heard that you and your Dad went to Cincinnati yesterday for the double-header. How did it go?" I instantly recognized that if I told them what actually had happened, not one of them would have believed me and I would have been the laughing stock of 26th Street going forward. So I only said, "It was great and the Dodgers are really good."

Very few friends of mine went away to college and no friends of mine went on to a seminary. That I ended up being the Bishop of the Episcopal Diocese of California was certainly bewildering to my old gang. If they had been aware in 1995 that I was venturing off into multiple cultures and beginning to work with people of indigenous tribes and competing religions, they would have been astonished. Upon my graduation from high school in Huntington in 1954, I only knew one Roman Catholic and had never had a conversation with an African-American or met a Native

American. I only knew white people and almost all of them were Protestant Christians. My only ethnic experience was having eaten in a Chinese restaurant four times.

They would not have been surprised that after two years at Kenyon College, in Gambier, Ohio, I received a letter from the college president stating that out of a class of 136 members, I ranked 126th academically. He encouraged the bottom 20 students not to return. Reading the letter carefully I noticed that he had not actually kicked me out. So I showed up on the first day of my junior year and sat on the front row waiting to be removed. No one seemed to notice, and I eventually graduated on time.

Years later, I was invited back to Kenyon to receive an honorary doctorate degree along with a former head of the Peace Corps and the comedian Jonathan Winters. One evening at dinner with them I mentioned my academic ineptitude. The former head of the Peace Corps thanked me for bringing that up. He said that he had only made it for one year at Kenyon. Then Jonathan broke in and said, "They kicked me out in February of my first year."

We looked at each other in wonder. Of all the students who made straight A's, why had they invited three dummies to return for honorary doctorate degrees? Actually, we came up with an answer.

Wasn't it great to fail when one is nineteen years old in front of your parents, peers and professors, and then to discover that life goes on, that the sun comes up again, and that there is much, much more ahead of you? Some people don't conspicuously fail until they are forty-five years old, and it devastates them. Fail early and get it over with. If you learn to deal with failure, you can raise teenagers and abide in intimate relationships. You can breathe again when you embrace failure as part of life, not as the determining moment of life.

The failures just kept on coming, to the surprise of no one who knew me back home. I almost didn't make it through the psychological test required before going to seminary. I had to take it three times. And then, in seminary, my bishop assigned me to two congregations where unquestionably I did a miserable job. Then, when I was ordained, the vestry (governing board) at my first church met, four months after my arrival, to decide whether or not to fire me. They said that I was the most immature clergyman they had encountered, that I had such a weak voice that it was hard to hear my sermons, and when they could hear, they weren't worth listening to. This meeting took place on the night that I brought my bride home from our honeymoon. The vote came out to a tie, six for firing me, and six for dismissing me. In the end a barber, Sam Simon, broke the tie, and everyone agreed that I needed discipline in sermon writing from a judge, a lawyer, and the senior priest. This protocol lasted for a year and a half until the bishop decided to send me elsewhere.

The place he sent me was the tiniest, poorest, dirtiest, most remote church, St. Thomas Episcopal Church, in the Diocese of West Virginia, whose congregation met in a former plumbing shop next to a steel mill in Weirton, West Virginia. Twenty people welcomed us in a building that held forty people, and on Palm Sunday, the ancient pump organ played the Indian Love Call, for reasons unknown. It was there that Mary and I arrived in the summer of 1963, and it was there that the light switch went on, the failures stopped, and the successes came one after another and never stopped. It all started when I talked everyone into having a Peach Festival. It was a spectacular winner and went on annually for fifty years. I discovered that I could rally the troops.

Far and away the most daring and pivotal thing I did was to pick up the phone in this one-company town and make an appointment with the president of Weirton Steel, Mr. Charles (Chuck) Tourney. Passing by several secretaries, I walked into his office, and he let me know that he was in a terrible hurry. Could I get right to the point! Abandoning all of my rehearsed lines, I blurted out that I was new to town and our church was $3,000 in debt. Without a word, he whipped out his checkbook and hurriedly wrote a check for that amount. He quickly said, "Is there anything else?" To which I instantly replied, "Yes there is. Would you and your wife come to our church and sit down in front?" He instantly agreed and asked if there was anything else. I said, "Yes. Since you and your wife are going to be members of the congregation, would you mind making a yearly pledge?" Close to exasperation, he said, "How much should that be?" When I said a thousand dollars, he wrote the check, but did not ask me if there was anything else. I walked out on the sidewalk and thought, "My goodness, I didn't know I had it in me. I think that I am an entrepreneur. I hope God can use an entrepreneur." At that moment my career took flight.

We loved being in Weirton and had a grand time with the people for our six years there. We were even able to buy three acres of land in a new downtown area, and build a brand new church building. I knew my star was rising when my bishop came for a visit and actually asked me, instead of telling me, about my next move. His two choices for me were at Martinsburg, W. Va., and St. Albans, W. Va. I demurred, saying that I would like to go home and talk this over with Mary. When she heard of it, she said that she wanted to go next to Washington, D.C., then to San Francisco, and finally to Paris. And then we had a big laugh. But within six months we were in Washington at St. Columba's Episcopal Church. Within ten years we ended up in San Francisco. And it turned out that we were in and out of Paris for decades. Looking back, I think that I married a prophetess.

In our ten years at St. Columba's in Washington, D.C., the congregation grew from 300 members to 2,000 members. It was a once-in-a-lifetime experience where the parish developed a spectacular education program for adults and children, an exquisite music program, marvelous traveling musical groups, and a deeply involved social ministries program. Plus engaged in lots of controversies over the Vietnam War, women's ordination, and the Watergate Crisis! We caught the full blast of the wind behind our backs and sailed forward confidently and swiftly. The folks back home in Weirton would not have been surprised. The folks back home in Wheeling and Huntington would have been shocked into disbelief.

In the winter of 1979, the mailman in Washington, D.C. delivered a large envelope from the Diocese of California stating that these people were looking for a new bishop and that my name was one of 171 nominees. If I chose to be a candidate, I would have to fill out a 19-page questionnaire. Since I had never been to California, and knew nothing about it, and cared nothing about it, I threw the packet in the garbage can. Later on, when I told Mary about it, she went to the garbage can, retrieved it, and read everything, even the last little paragraph about the final 24 candidates—and their spouses—being flown to San Francisco for an interview. Mary looked at me and said, "Fill it out!"

I filled it out in January 1979, and soon Mary and I were in San Francisco for an interview. Before returning home to Washington on a red-eye, we settled on a bench in Union Square to enjoy the sweet sunshine of a California day. Looking around, we spotted a man working on an ice sculpture. A TV camera crew was interviewing patrons of the park. And almost everyone had prophylactics on their fingers. I inquired what this was all about and was told that this was National Condom Week in San Francisco. I mentioned that in Washington, D.C. we had National Secretaries Week, and I asked if this were anything like that. I was told, "We are number one in the nation in syphilis and number three in gonorrhea. So we are encouraging condom use." Then, when we were told that the ice sculpture was of a gonorrhea germ, I apologized for not noticing that right off. Once we boarded the airplane, Mary said, "Who in the world wants to be the bishop of Sodom and Gomorrah?" The folks back home would have understood that response.

On a Friday afternoon in early March 1979, a telephone call from San Francisco announced that I was chosen (at age 42) to be one of the six final candidates and asked if I would agree to stand for election. I immediately turned down the honor, remembering the scene in Union Square and thinking about our teenage children and their youth groups. "Would you think about the decision over the weekend, and let us call you back on Monday?" was the question. "No harm in that," was my answer. Then three quite unusual things happened.

First, on Saturday, I received a letter from Santa Clara, California informing me that seventeen people wanted to vote for me for bishop. I knew none of these people, and had never heard of their parish. Second, on Sunday morning as I was striding through the hallway of St. Columba's Church to start the adult class, a lady got off a bench, came over, grabbed me by my coat, and said, "I have flown all the way from California to say three words to you. 'Don't Back Out.'" Third, at the 11:15 a.m. service, I baptized the nephew of Henry and Nancy Kissinger. Afterwards, they invited Mary and me to lunch at their home in Georgetown. We obviously accepted, and at lunch I asked Dr. Kissinger what he was going to do with the rest of his life. After a long answer in his strong German accent, he asked the same question of me. As I explained my current situation, he dropped his salad fork onto his plate and said, "Mr. Swing, you mean to tell me that California's last two bishops had tragic careers and you have had abundant success, but you will not be a candidate because you want your children in a good youth group?!? Mr. Swing, that is not responsible leadership!" Afterwards Mary and I staggered out onto the sidewalk in Georgetown, looked at each other and knew exactly the right thing to do. The folks at our home parish of St. Columba's would understand our decision.

Later, when I was bishop of California in San Francisco, our church hospital, St. Luke's, fell on hard financial times. We were losing between $20 and $25 million year after year, and no one would partner with us, or take us under their wing. I pleaded with the Board of St. Luke's Hospital to stay in business. Then I got in my car, drove to Sacramento and begged the head of Sutter Health to adopt us. They did. And eventually, as a Sutter affiliate, St. Luke's began the process of building a new hospital.

When the Diocese of California didn't have a true conference center, I appointed a Board of Directors for the Bishop's Ranch, hired a Director, and raised enough money to buy over 300 acres of land in Sonoma County, where we built or renovated several buildings.

After the so-called Rodney King riots in California in 1992, leaders of the African-American Episcopalians group met in my living room to try to figure out an appropriate, meaningful response to poverty among members of the African-American community. The consensus was to start a bank, a capital development bank. So I became a banker and eventually, our bank in Oakland, California was capitalized for $37 million.

When the AIDS pandemic broke out and San Francisco was an epicenter, I hosted the world's first religious response conference to the crisis. People from forty-four states and four nations showed up. I ended up speaking about AIDS to the whole world over and served on the Board of the American Foundation for AIDS Research for twenty years.

On January 1, 1983, I housed and fed 40 homeless people in the basement of that Cathedral, and brought down the wrath of the neighborhood. Now, thirty years later, programs sponsored by the Episcopal Diocese of California house 1,500 homeless every night in eleven locations, serve 280,000 meals a year, and have a $20 million budget.

There were also responses to the Loma Prieta Earthquake and Oakland Hills Fire, and the ministries to gays and lesbians (later broadened to the LGBT community). And there were many other conspicuous and quiet innovations of ministry.

All of this and much more was on the line on June 30, 1995 as I sat with six other people in my living room at 9:00 a.m. I wondered what the diocese would think when I told everyone that I was actually committing myself to led in the creation of a United Religions. I would no longer merely be a catalyst. I would be the fundraiser, the spokesperson, the world traveler, the target of discontent, and the risk-taker-in-chief.

And I wondered if this was the bridge too far. Would this be the occasion of harm to my family and to the diocese? My guess was that the diocese was satisfied enough by the convincing-enough argument I had made for a United Religions that they would cut me some slack. As for my family? That is a topic for a later chapter. What will the folks back home think? We would see.

Chapter 6
Stenciled Together

When Mary and I lived near the smoke stacks of the steel mills in West Virginia, if the wind was blowing in our direction at night, we would wake up in the morning and the outline of our heads would be stenciled on our pillows. We would shut the windows tightly and lock them, and we drew closed the curtains in front of the windows. Nonetheless, the tiny ferrous particles made an undeterred path to our pillows. Mary and I became stenciled in steel. I carry that picture in my mind because it captures our life together.

Mary Willis Taylor was born in Richmond, Virginia where she attended a private Episcopal School, St. Catherine's, and was a debutante of that city. Upon graduation from Sweet Briar College, also in Virginia, she worked in Silver Springs, Maryland as a mathematician for the Johns Hopkins Applied Physics Laboratory on a Navy contract to perform war games. When I was a seminarian in Alexandria, Virginia, just across the Potomac River from D.C., we met on a blind date. Mary was living in Georgetown, around the corner from Jack and Jackie Kennedy. (Later, I was an usher at his inauguration and seated people on the Senate side, just a few yards from where he said, "Ask not what your country can do for you...")

When we became engaged, one difficulty was where to go on the honeymoon. Her girlfriends had gone to Europe or Bermuda on their honeymoons. These destinations were way out of my pocketbook range. Then a brilliant idea dawned. How about the Island of Nantucket? It was off the coast and sounded exotic. So we wrote for a brochure of where we might stay. Clearly, the best place was Emmons Corners, but it was frightfully expensive. So I wrote a letter to Mr. Emmons saying that we would love to say there—but! By airmail, special delivery came a reply from Mr. Emmons stating that we could stay on our financial terms, that he would meet us at the airport, and that we could have a little rose-covered cottage with a fireplace and a kitchen behind Emmons Corners. Thirty-three years later, Mary and I returned to Nantucket looking for Emmons Corners, but it was gone. Then she went down one street and I down another looking for our rose-covered cottage. She yelled that she had found it, and indeed she had. When I ran up, there it was—but no longer a rose-covered cottage. Now it was a fast food takeout joint. But—its name was "Mary's Hot To Go." It was time to take a picture.

October was always our month. We met on October 7, 1959. We had our first date on October 7, 1960 and we were married on October 7, 1961. (It was fifteen years later before we connected these dots.) And finally our first born, Alice Marshall Swing, was born on October 23, 1962 in Wheeling, West Virginia in the middle of the Cuban Missile Crisis. As a matter of fact, on the day of her birth, the Wheeling Intelligencer newspaper ran this headline: "Kennedy Prohibits All Deliveries in the Western Hemisphere." Regardless of our president's mandate, Alice was delivered.

When I was given full responsibility for a church in Weirton, W. Va., Mary changed the culture of the place with her hospitality. Many picnics and dinners followed. She did the same in Washington, D.C. To augment my salary, she worked at various jobs: as a secretary, as the Manager of the National Cathedral's College of Preachers, as the cofounder of a business to make clothes for women clergy, as an employee of an investment firm, as a development officer for a school, and finally, after earning a certificate in financial planning from the University of California, Berkeley Extension, she was a partner with a firm providing financial services.

All along the way we had great adventures, some earthy, some regal. In West Virginia, I started a ministry at Waterford Park Race Track for the jockeys, hot-walkers, trainers, and their families. No offering was ever taken, but they gave me tips on the races. So Mary and I would get a baby sitter, go to the racetrack, have dinner, and bet from the suggested list. A lot of the time we made enough money to pay for the evening. On other nights, the results encouraged us to tighten our belts and not to pay so much attention to sure things.

The move to California had not been a sure thing for Mary. In fact, she said that the Grand Canyon must have been dug by the heels of Virginia girls who balked at having to move to California. Also, she was so homesick after our move that she just had to take a weekend off and go away and think about it. Think about what it meant to be a Californian, a San Franciscan, and the wife of a bishop who is constantly on the road, with her raising two teenage children without any support system. I had a ready-made constituency; she was just lonely. This was a monumentally hard move for her.

But there turned out to be lots of benefits to offset the challenges. In February 1983, the Master of the Household of Her Majesty, Queen Elizabeth II, invited us aboard H. M. Yacht Britannia for a celebration of President and Mrs. Reagan's 35th wedding Anniversary. (Another time, we shared a room in London that was so bad a rat was trying to gnaw his way out.) President George H. W. Bush and his wife, Barbara, hosted us for a weekend at Camp David. Mary and I slept on the floor of a jungle in Papua, New Guinea while on an errand of charity. Elizabeth Taylor invited us to her sixtieth birthday party in the same year that Mother Teresa invited us for a visit in Calcutta.

Together we spent ten years commuting from San Francisco to Jerusalem and then eight more years commuting from San Francisco to China on companion relationships among Christians. And we ran with the golf crowd at the Bing Crosby (later "AT&T") Pebble Beach, National Pro-Am Golf Tournament. Moreover, there were meetings of the House of Bishops and General Conventions of the Episcopal Church, which we attended all over the United States. Our heads have been stenciled on many a bed.

But what about taking out a line of credit for one million dollars in 1996 in order to fund the start of the United Religions Initiative? Mary knew full well what it meant for her to put her signature beside mine on the official documents. It might put us in debt for the rest of our lives. It would definitely have an impact on our marriage and our family. Yet, she signed on. Why? Because she had traveled enough, heard enough, seen enough to imagine that a United Religions or a United Religions Initiative could happen. She believed in the vision and trusted me and herself.

When the URI office opened in 1996, Mary was URI's first Financial Officer, and she did that job as a volunteer for several years. She traveled hundreds of thousands of miles on missions taking the lumps, arranging travel plans while in motion, and keeping operations together. In addition, she held countless parties of fun and fundraising, and these contributed greatly in keeping URI afloat and solvent. It could be said about a few people, but most definitely it should be said that without Mary Swing, there would be no URI.

From 2011 through 2013, Mary lost the top of one lung to cancer, had breast cancer and radiation for it, lost the top her other lung to cancer, and had 15 weeks of chemotherapy. Not once did she cave in to self-pity, but always kept imagining a better day.

Thankfully, that better day arrived in the spring of 2014, when she was proclaimed cancer free and came back to normal vigor and activity. Her valiant nature is stenciled on the history of URI, and now the outline of her head is no longer defined by ferrous products, but by returning hair and by a smile that melts me.

Chapter 7
The Great Journey to Recruit Religious Leaders to Support a United Religions

The first stop on my world tour was New York City, where I spoke to religious Non-Governmental Organizations at the United Nations. I addressed a formal session of these representatives of the world's major religions and interfaith organizations. Dr. Robert Traer, who was the Secretary General of the International Association for Religious Freedom (IARF), was tasked with countering my vision of a United Religions. Since he had first hand experience of international interfaith work on the ground, he was able to find many of the flaws in my proposal for a United Religions. Nevertheless, I captured the enthusiastic support of almost all the religious representatives present. It was a good prelude to a world tour.

The time came for what would be the greatest adventure of my life. On February 5, 1996, Mary and I left from the San Francisco Airport. Armed with the skeleton of an itinerary to India, Pakistan, Mauritius, Egypt, England and Italy, we boarded our plane carrying small brochures that advertised that a United Religions was on the horizon. The brochures advertised that the proposed United Religions would be built on four basic attributes: a symbol of unity among religions; a spiritual resource for the sake of the world; a collective voice to speak from spiritual roots to the world's issues; and a channel for common action, especially among the grassroots people of religions, and primarily in the field of conflict resolution. In the brochures, there was an optimistic timeline for implementation. Also, in the Presidio of San Francisco, four large buildings were about to be available at Fort Scott; I built in the expectation of renting these buildings to be the physical anchor of the coming United Religions. I had to paint some kind of coherent picture to start the conversation about a United Religions, and the brochure was it.

Very little was firm on our three-month sabbatical trip. First off, I would preach at the Mar Thoma Convention in South India, and for that, my airfare and Mary's were paid. Then, thanks to Marcus Braybrooke, I had been asked to give a major address at an interfaith gathering in Oxford, England. He arranged our room and board there as well.

As for meeting leading religious leaders, I had only three solid appointments lined up. One was with the Dalai Lama in India, one with Senator Javid Iqbal in Lahore, Pakistan, and the other with the Orthodox Ecumenical Patriarch in Turkey. There was an outside chance that, while on the road, I could tie down appointments with the Archbishop of Canterbury, with the Inter-Religious Cardinal at the Vatican, and with Dr. Karin Singh in Calcutta. Beyond that, I had audacious hopes of meeting such leaders as the Muslim Sheikh of Al-Azhar, Mother Teresa, a Chief Rabbi in Israel, and the Hindu Shankaracharya of Kanchipuram, but I lacked an entrée to them and my status as a religious leader was slight at best. So I began with a bare bones schedule, little money, only a faint idea about how to get from place to place, and no planned support along the way except for what Mary and her new, 1996 model computer could provide. The entire thing was a leap of faith.

First stop, Southern India. On February 7, 1996, Mary and I got off the plane with two large suitcases and four carry-ons in Cochin, India, where we expected to be picked up by the people with whom we had corresponded for the past six months. But no one was there in that blisteringly hot airport. We sat for hours on our luggage and since no one spoke English, we sat quietly. At last, a little man in a yellow-orange suit emblazoned with a large, cheerful badge came and asked: "Bishop?" I leapt toward him in relief. When I turned to introduce my wife to him, the look on his face indicated that I was the wrong kind of bishop. It turned out that the Roman Catholics were having a convention in that area, and his job was to pick up dignitaries at the airport. So we got back to waiting. Finally someone came to the airport who spoke English and who helped us call the convention organizers. More waiting. Eventually two men arrived and took us to a nearby town and told us to stay there for two days. Ah, no one could have had a more breathtaking introduction to the life in the fast lane of international interfaith work.

Actually, we only stayed at the hotel for a day, and at daybreak on the second day, we were driven to a spot of the Pamba River bank where the Maramon Convention of the Mar Thoma Church would take place on a large sandbar. For seven days there would be Bible Study in small groups at 7:00 a.m. At 10:00 a.m. there would be a two-hour service on the riverbank for 150,000 people. In the afternoon, the big service started at 2:00 p.m. and was attended by 200,000 people. And then in the evening, there was a little service for 85,000 people. All sermons lasted one hour: thirty minutes in English and thirty minutes of translation. There were five of us preachers and we were working day and night. The audience was deeply literate in Holy Scripture and expected substantive, Biblically-based sermons. I had never been so immersed in the Bible since I had been in seminary. Mary and I were accustomed to conventions where issues were debated and resolutions had to be addressed, budgets were past and strategies were laid out. So

Mary asked a local bishop if this Maramon Convention would be addressing the business of the church, and he said, "Our business is preaching the Gospel and evangelizing, and that's all that happens at the Maramon."

So we retired to our room in the jungle to search the Scripture. We found concrete walls, a beautiful wooden door, tile flooring, two dim lights that worked a few times a day, one chair, one desk, two beds, a ceiling fan (which also worked occasionally), a concrete bathroom, toilet and sink, and 618 mosquitoes.

These people, the Mar Thoma (named after St. Thomas, who allegedly visited this part of India), used to be part of the Syrian Orthodox Church, but because of a split over how much access lay people should have to the Bible, they left and became thoroughly evangelical without becoming thoroughly Protestant. They are sort of a hybrid of ancient and modern, and today they number over a million people worldwide. They are obviously very ecumenical (open to all Christians), and now I would test to see if they were very interfaith-oriented (open to Muslims, Hindus, Jews and all religions).

This test came unexpectedly, at 7:00 a.m. Bible study for about 100 people on the edge of the jungle. I was speaking into a microphone and had no idea of how many people, not visibly present, were listening as well. I was making a point that Jesus seemed to have an open and appreciative attitude to people of other religions and cultures, and I cited the story of the Good Samaritan, where the hero was not of Jesus' faith, and the story of the Syro-Phoenician woman who, despite not being of Jesus' faith, was the heroine of the important story. Following on these stories I mentioned in passing that I was just beginning a world pilgrimage to create a United Religions. A large, ferocious verbal confrontation ensued. People started clambering out of the jungle with Bibles in hand stating that salvation came only through Jesus, that Jesus only pitied people of other faiths, and that I should be at their Maramon only encouraging them to convert Hindus and Muslims, not to figure out how to live happily with them. "Who is Jesus Christ for you?" was a common question. After that, my translator tried always to mute my messages before they reached the ears of the folks.

So it all started. I had to dig down much deeper into myself to answer the question of who Jesus Christ is for me. I wasn't undone by the confrontation. As a matter of fact I welcomed it. Heated exchanges followed that leapt over into politics, religion and Indian history. I took them on toe to toe. I was soon interviewed by local newspapers, and the prospect of a United Religions hit the front pages. Religion was a big deal in Southern India.

I quickly recognized that what I was saying was received with mixed reviews among the congregation of 200,000—but what about the bishops? These celibate, simple-living, hospitable, generous men of such clear and decent character, what were they thinking? I never found out until ten years later when they took positions of leadership in URI India. What a revelation! But in 1996 I assumed that I had only succeeded in alienating the entire Mar Thoma Church from the movement for a United Religions. When I asked Metropolitan Alexander if the Mar Thoma Church could endorse the concept of a United Religions, he said that the bishops would have to study it further and watch how it grew.

Also he said something that I wanted to tuck away to think about on another day. He said, "We are Indians first. The people of India see the earth here as Mother Goddess from which comes life and food, so we have great affection for India."

At this time in my trip, I was reading several books while traveling and one of them was Laurens Van Der Post's *About Blady*. In it, someone delivered a smashingly good speech, to which the hero replied, "...eloquently said, now let's get back to cultivating our garden." The interminable interfaith meetings I would be attending around the world in the next years would turn out to be ninety-nine percent speeches and one percent action. I vowed to myself that whatever UR or URI turned out to be, it had to be ninety-nine percent action and one percent talking.

Among the enormous throng of people on the riverbank there was one man listening who would one day put URI on the map in this part of India and in lots of places around the world. He was Abraham Karickam, an Indian educator, who unbeknownst to me, positively understood the URI message and was ready to throw himself and his considerable organizational gifts into action. I was leaving the Maramon feeling like I had done a decent job of preaching and a questionable job in generating support for the coming United Religions, and on the whole, feeling kind of a failure. On the last day, when I went to put some money into the offering bag at church, a lizard jumped out of the bag and landed on my chest. Later, when I went to brush my teeth, a five-inch scorpion came out of the drain and stared at me. Perhaps it was time to move on.

I could not have had a more exciting, eye-opening, challenging start. I did not achieve an official endorsement for a United Religions from these religious leaders, but I received a greater gift. The Mar Thoma leaders were intrigued with the concept and were willing to back it in a secondary fashion, with generous hospitality. As it turned out, that is exactly what I needed desperately.

Mary and I had many days to go until a solid appointment, so here we were stranded again in Southern India. Without us saying a word about our marooned state, the Mar Thoma leaders reached out to arrange the details to make our wildest dreams of interviews in this part of India come true. I was hoping against hope to meet the Hindu leader, the Shankaracharya of Kanchipuram, the global interfaith leader Dr. Karin Singh, and Mother Teresa in Southern India. There had been no response from them to our attempts to arrange appointments. It was at that precise moment that we were told by the Mar Thoma officials that they would take us under their wings.

Chapter 8
The Great Journey—
The Surprise of Hospitality

A trip to Madras (now known as Chennai) had not been on our itinerary or in our imaginations, but our new Mar Thoma friends knew that it was essential for us to get there. So they guided Mary in purchasing the airline tickets, got us to the Cochin Airport, and had their colleagues pick us up in Madras, India's fourth largest city with about ten million people.

We were met by Father Mathew, a mathematician who had been a priest for just one year, assisting in his parish of 800. We were also met by Joji, who runs the bishop's residence and office. We drove through their sprawling city and saw lots of Hindu temples. We arrived at the bishop's residence in the Anna Nagar, which is the largest residential area in Asia. A very nice looking house, it was a Hindu residence and so had a Hindu deity on the front wall. It became apparent that Father Mathew and Joji were instructed to do everything possible for us. Soon a neighbor, Philipose, owner of a tire factory, came over with his wife. It was a bizarre comedy as Matthew and Joji were on the phone changing our Lahore flight (extending it by a day), getting hotel rooms in Calcutta and Delhi, getting people to pick us up at airports, while Philipose kept yelling at them to get us Pepsis and papaya and cookies, and on and on. Then they did our laundry and made dinner for us. Madras has a milder climate than Kerala, but its mosquito population is much larger. I killed twenty-five mosquitoes and went to sleep.

The following morning after prayers, we were whisked away to the elegant home of a prominent Hindu lawyer, P. Hadras, who joined us for a trip to Kanchipuram so that, as I understood, we would at least get a glimpse of the beautiful temple there as well as the famous Vedanta ashram of the Shankaracharya.

During the 73-kilometer drive, we had briefings on the Hindu faith and on the reason Christians are in disfavor among many in India—namely, that in 1947, while the Hindus were great patriots and fighters for India, the Christians had lingering loyalties to the English "enslavers." The four Shankaracharyas, leaders of Hinduism, are located at four compass points: North, East, South, and West. Kanchipuram is the seat of the leader in the South. Also, the drive afforded enough time for me to explain my United Religions proposal to P. Hadras. He explained to me that we would actually be meeting the Shankaracharya in a few minutes.

What a scene! The car stopped in front of a dirty and heavily-populated place. We were told to take off our shoes. First we went up some stairs and entered a room, where, to our right, men were working busily setting bars in place for a monkey cage. Then we went to another room and downstairs to the outside, where an elephant was standing. We trudged down an alleyway and through a doorway into a room full of people. A large number of hyperactive monkeys hissed and played near a shrine. Then we stopped in a room that only had a few mats and a man in a chair wearing an orange-colored robe, a man who had his back to us. He was chatting through an opening in the wall to people going by, and giving them a marking of some sort on their foreheads—blessings in the form of a powder. This was The

Shankaracharya of Kanchipuram! The holy man who spoke seven languages fluently! I was told to sit on the floor cross-legged at his feet, and to begin speaking about the United Religions. He turned around, read my brochure, and asked me about the symbols of the different religions on our stationery. I blushed. I had no idea what they meant.

During my presentation he occasionally laughed and once in a while he laughed heartily. It was only later that I learned that holy men laugh when they hear something that they think is true. When it seems that the truth is deeply in line with the stars, they laugh heartily. At the time, hearing him laugh was somewhat puzzling and slightly disturbing, but he became excited about the concept of a United Religions and endorsed it. Furthermore, he promised to send a delegation to the Charter Writing Conference in San Francisco the following year. As he draped a necklace of cloves and cardamom around my neck, he encouraged me to make sure that the Sufi Muslims were invited. In my wildest dreams, I could not have imagined such a response from this most Holy man of Hinduism.

But the Mar Thoma hosts were not finished. Within a day they had us in Calcutta in the care of Mr. P. M. John, a Mar Thoma lay leader and businessman, and his family.

He met us at the airport. The highway into town was the first straight, one-way, two-lane road that we'd seen in India. The Muslims were celebrating the end of Ramadan; the Chinese were celebrating their New Year. We arrived in the center of town on a main drag at a grand old English building with beggars sleeping out front, a Muslim elevator operator, 16-foot ceilings, and, finally, a beautifully decorated apartment. We went to bed at midnight but never slept because our windows were just over the traffic, which was combustive and constant.

On Ash Wednesday, February 21, 1996, after family devotions, they found out that Dr. Karan Singh was in town and staying at the Taj Bengal Hotel. Earlier, in the United States, someone who brags that he knows lots of famous people and could fix me up with timely appointments, assured me that I had an appointment with the famous Dr. Karan Singh. But when it came right down to it and I was in India, Karan Singh had never heard of me. When my Mar Thoma friends spoke with Karan Singh's people, they agreed that he would stop in the hotel lobby for a minute on his way to an important meeting and meet with me.

Who is Dr. Karan Singh? At birth, he was heir to the throne of Jammu and Kashmir. At age eighteen he was made regent and later head of the Indian State of Jammu and Kashmir. Still later, he became governor of this region. The list of his vocations, accomplishments, and honors is quite long. For me, the important thing was that he was a recognized global interfaith leader of considerable merit. Like many other leaders in India, he had spent a great deal of time thinking about the necessity of a United Religions, and he anticipated the day of its formation.

Elegantly and haughtily, he breezed into the hotel lobby and let me know that my time with him was to be extremely brief. Despite this, we actually covered a lot of ground.

It was evident from our conversation that he had thought about a United Religions many times on earlier occasions, and thus he was led to ask the obvious questions about how to choose representatives, where they would meet, and other particulars. Interestingly, he told me that great religious leaders are not great spiritual people and that I was wasting my time pursuing famous religious leaders. Then almost laughingly he told me, me from West Virginia, that I should seek out the gurus of Yogaville, West Virginia. In the end, he wondered out loud if perhaps this was the time to strike for a United Religions, and if perhaps I might be the person to lead the way to this eventuality. And "in a cloud of dust" he was gone. Whew! I had interviewed two out of the three on my list in Southern India. Also, it became clear that the idea of a United Religions made primarily of spiritual sages of each tradition rather than religious leaders of each tradition was an idea that deserved future consideration.

We got our first American newspapers in two weeks in the Taj Bengal—the Indian state of Bengal. The other Bengal has since become Bangladesh. While waiting for our host to pick us up, we saw trees across the road from the hotel full of bats with wingspans of four to five feet.

At the Maramon, the word had spread in the Mar Thoma community that I cared deeply about social ministries. So just as they had in Kerala, the Mar Thoma showed me their social ministries in Calcutta. Chief among these was a place called ANTARA. In 1980, the Mar Thoma Church had gone out of town, bought a large farm and started a medical facility. To this they added a facility for the mentally ill, then a residency program for drug and alcohol dependency. Everyone was involved working, participating in farming, or carpentry, or making envelopes. It was glorious, and it was now sponsored not only by the Mar Thomas, but also by Muslims, Hindus, Armenian Orthodox, an Episcopal diocese in Illinois, and Mother Teresa.

Ah, Calcutta and Mother Teresa! How to get to her? Leave it to the Mar Thoma people. Actually, the wife of our host, P.M. John, worked closely with Mother Teresa in the ANTARA ministry, so she and Mother Teresa were good friends. Mrs. John arranged the meeting. As darkness set in on our second day in Calcutta, we were driven to a little alley where we got out and walked until we came to an old building with a tiny sign that said in faded letters simply, "Mother Teresa." We knocked on the door and were escorted past a large number of bustling nuns, across an atrium exposed to the night air, up some stairs, and into a hallway where we took off our shoes and sat on a bench. As the nuns filed past us into a chapel, Mother Teresa burst forth in her blue habit and tennis shoes, eighty-six years old, with the energy of a fourteen-year-old, standing probably four feet six inches and weighing about eighty pounds. She grabbed my hand and looked me straight in the eye while we chatted for half an hour. At first, we spent a great deal of time talking about the ministry to people with AIDS, each comparing stories of what we had done and were doing. When I told her about the United Religions, she was elated and promised to get all of her official and semi-official colleagues in 120 countries praying for its success. Not only did she endorse the idea, she said that she would talk to the Pope about it when she next saw him, in a couple of months. At the end, we prayed together and exchanged blessings. She walked us over to get our shoes, giving us respectful farewells until we were down the stairs. The event was a spiritual privilege of the first order.

Afterwards, we were driven to the Mar Thoma Church in Calcutta where we visited next door in the home of the priest and his wife. On the walls of their living room were two items: a picture of Jesus and a picture of Dennis the Menace taken from the author, Hank Ketcham's book, *Prayers and Graces.*

Actually it was a delightful book, mostly about the 23rd Psalm. That book had not one but two forewords, one by Billy Graham and his wife Ruth, and one by me. Hank was an old golfing buddy and friend, so I had happily obliged and was honored to do so. I promised the children of the house, Debbie and Dan, that I would send them a copy of the whole book when I got back to San Francisco. In Calcutta I was reminded of what a small world it is.

There is no way that this pilgrimage could have been nearly as rich and complete without the surprise of hospitality that was offered spontaneously by the Mar Thoma leaders. Eventually, when the Charter of URI was written in 1999, the sixth principle said, "We give and receive hospitality." I learned how essential that was for interfaith work when Mary and I were guided around Southern India by our new friends.

Chapter 9
The Great Journey—The Dalai Lama and So Much More

In the shuttle relay of Mar Thoma friends handing us off to one another across India, we arrived in New Delhi with two solid appointments in hand: one with Senator Javid Iqbal in Lahore, Pakistan and the other with His Holiness the Dalai Lama in Dharamsala, India. Our newest Mar Thoma friends had corralled Zoroastrian leaders, who scheduled several speaking engagements for me. It was all very exciting as both groups worked to have me meet new people and witness the interfaith yearnings of unexpected people.

Our first stop in New Delhi was at the Baha'i Temple. I was not prepared for such beauty and size. Until now I had thought of Baha'i as a small, persecuted group, so I was expecting a humble campus with a few little buildings. Instead I encountered a magnificent temple that hosted 25,000 visitors a day (more than the Eiffel Tower and Statue of Liberty combined). Plus there were nine pools and extensive gardens. Incidentally the Baha'i have no sermons, but in their worship services they read from the Holy Scriptures of various religious traditions. I figured that these people would be sympathetic to the United Religions idea, and when I spoke with their leaders at the temple, sure enough, they responded positively and wanted to be part of the Charter Writing Conference the following year in San Francisco.

I tried to see the great man, Gyani Sahib Singh, at the Bangla Sahib Gurudwara, the most prominent Sikh house of worship in Delhi, but he was out of town. So I went for a visit to the Gurudwara and spoke with (actually, listened to) the leaders who were on duty. Thousands and thousands of people were present on just an ordinary day. The whole scene was profoundly impressive.

That night, Mary and I went out to dinner by ourselves for the first time in a month.

The next day, an unforeseeable thing happened. I asked a cab-driver to tell me what was the biggest Muslim mosque in New Delhi, and he said it was the gigantic Jama Masjid (mosque). But he advised me not go there looking for an interview with the Imam, Syed Ahmed Bukhari (also known as Naib Shahih Imam), who had a reputation of being fiery and controversial. My interest piqued, I asked the driver to take me immediately to the mosque. I arrived during prayers, and when I told a guard about my intention to talk with the Imam, he took me down some stairs to an office where apples, oranges, and other edibles were laid out. Then a tall, menacing man appeared, explaining that he was the Imam's interpreter and educating me on the difference between the Sunni of this mosque and the Shias from other mosques. Soon Bukhari appeared, a short man with darting eyes and great intensity. When I explained to him about the coming United Religions, he said, "Wouldn't that be wonderful? We could meet each other for the first time and speak from the heart. And instead of the United Nations talking to us, the religious people, we could talk to the United Nations and tell those people what we think." He endorsed the United Religions idea and wanted to be posted on developments so that his people could be at the Charter Writing table.

As great as this visit was, there was another one that topped it. A local Mar Thoma priest took me to the hospital room of Metropolitan Bishop Paulose Mar Gregorios, the first bishop of the Delhi diocese of the Indian Orthodox Church, who was trying to recover from a stroke. Who was this man? He had been Emperor Haile Selassie's Secretary and his Education Advisor in Ethiopia. He had been President of the World Council of Churches in Geneva. He was on the Board of the Parliament of World Religions in Chicago. He was a Professor of Systematic Theology in Syria. No one in the interfaith world was held in higher esteem. I had not dreamed of meeting him, and was thrilled to do so.

You can bet that he had never heard of me. Nevertheless, when I showed him the brochure of the Coming United Religions, he expressed a very strong positive reaction. In fact, his was the strongest positive reaction to United Religions that I was ever to receive. He sparkled in response, dissecting each sentence historically and through several academic dimensions. He remembered that the General Secretary of the United Nations, U Thant, had come through India in 1953 advocating a United Religions. U Thant had stated that the United Nations was not equipped to produce the unity that the world needed, but a United Religions might. Gregorios urged me not to let the United Religions become merely a symbol. "It needs to be an agent of global unity," he said. Gregorios loved talking about the United Religions and he had anticipated its day for a long time. I left town the next day, and sadly, Metropolitan Gregorios died a few months later. Nevertheless, he had signaled to me that I was on the right path and should be bold in introducing the idea of a United Religions.

Going from India to Pakistan, two neighboring nuclear enemies, was an odd experience, beginning on the plane where I listened to a prayer of Mohammed piped aboard. A flight attendant pulled me aside and asked a host of questions. Then in flight, someone appeared next to me, spilled coffee on me, and offered a napkin from his tray, which held his uneaten meal. I felt like I was being scrutinized. And when we got to

Pakistan, we never went through customs. Our passports, which had been confiscated along with our luggage, simply arrived at the house where we were staying. For all of this activity, there was a clear explanation. We were guests of Senator Javid Iqbal, who was one of our keynote speakers at the 1995 Youth Conference prior to the U.N. 50th celebration, and was the son of one of the most influential Pakistanis at the birth of the country.

What was I doing in Pakistan? There was no chance to meet a famous religious leader. And, as a matter of fact, I would not be talking with one grassroots person. My conversations were solely held with members of the Pakistani intelligentsia and social elite. I had not the foggiest notion of how that could possibly be of help in the creation of a United Religions, but I was intrigued with the prospect of visiting Pakistan.

A couple of years earlier, when I was choosing speakers from various major religions for the Youth Conference of 1995, I had a list of potential Muslim speakers, mostly famous imams. Not well informed or the least bit strategic, I chose to pursue Javid Iqbal, who at the time was a member of the Supreme Court of Pakistan and most certainly not a religious leader. Now Mary and I were about to stay in the home of Javid's friend, Ambassador Syed Amjad Ali, for four days in Lahore.

The whole stay was dream-like. Syed Amjad Ali had sat at the famous "Indian Round Table" with Mahatma Gandhi in 1930-31; had been Pakistan's first Ambassador to the United States, and later Ambassador to the United Nations, and had a distinguished career. We luxuriated in the endlessly long rooms of his home, his oriental rugs, and twenty-five-foot ceilings. We had our eyes opened at lunch on the veranda with members of the Supreme Court, industrialists, scholars, and a host of others. Amjad Ali's sister, Kishwar, had a dinner party for us and invited journalists, ambassadors, a school principal, and a U.N. representative just back from working in Iraq with the Kurds. In addition, Javid Iqbal and his wife, Nasira, a prominent lawyer, had a dinner party for us, and those present included the American Consul General, a bishop of the Church of Pakistan, the Speaker of the Pakistani Party, and the U.S. Information Chief. There are no more generous and thoughtful hosts in the world than the Pakistanis. Wow, we were light years away from the Pamba River of last week.

Javid's wife was involved in an interfaith initiative hosted by His Royal Highness King Hussein of Jordan and the Duke of Edinburgh, and she promised to put in a good word about United Religions. Barbar, the brother of Syed Amjad Ali, was also involved and promised to ask Prince Charles if he would send someone to the Charter Writing Session of United Religions next year. This raised further hope in me that it all might just happen. Prominent people of the world gather to do interfaith work. They are a rarefied group that has a unique perspective and opportunity.

One afternoon on the front porch of Syed Amjad Ali's house, someone from the Bay Area who was studying languages in Lahore joined the group. His name was Amogalilidos ("call me Alan") and was much involved in the Host Committee of the URI group in San Francisco. He wanted to take me to meet a famous Muslim scholar. So we walked for a couple of miles, went down a narrow, dirty street, knocked on a door, walked by piles of books in a hallway, and found a little man with thick glasses hunched over a manuscript. Alan introduced me and the old man said with considerable force, "You are with the CIA!" And that was that.

In all of these conversations, I was learning about the country, the literacy rate, politics, law, and culture, but not much about religion. Javid's famous father, Hakeem-ul-Ummat Iqbal, the spiritual leader of Pakistan's birth, lies in state in a mausoleum outside the famous Badshahi Mosque of Pakistan, and his spiritual poems are still popular and relevant. But I was outside the religious life of the country. The closest I came was when I visited a local spiritual leader and politician, Qazi Hussain Ahmad, who kept losing elections and frightening people. I could see why as I entered his compound, with fifteen-foot brick walls and men with Uzis lining every step of my way. But once inside with Qazi Hussain, I had a grand conversation with him about the United Religions. He got so excited that he made me a map of the world and gave the names of Islamic leaders that I needed to contact. He told me that I needed to stop in Egypt and visit his best friend who was the leader of the Egyptian fundamentalists. Figuring that I wanted to stay away from more weapons, I said that my schedule was full and that the best way forward would be for me to send them some brochures. The next morning in the Lahore newspaper it reported that, "seven hardened criminals with sophisticated weapons" were arrested and confessed to being hired to murder leaders of the Muslim Party and to attack Qazi Hussain Ahmad's fortress. That convinced me not to revisit Qazi Hussain that day.

Unbeknownst to me, there was in Lahore a Roman Catholic Dominican priest, Father James Channan, who was a friend of Javid Iqbal and who would one day make sure that Pakistan would be the third most URI-populated nation in the world. Eventually, he and I would become like brothers. What seemed on the surface to be an educational and social trip actually turned out to be an inadvertent laying of the groundwork for spectacular URI growth in a country that greatly needed interfaith understanding.

As we were flying back to New Delhi for a madcap twenty-four-hour stay, I was convinced that I was onto something big. Not everyone, but certainly a preponderance of people that I met genuinely entertained the idea of a United Religions and did not immediately dismiss it out of hand. Of course, we were in a part of the world where religion was not only an integral part of life and language; it was a part of the world which had suffered severely from religious hostilities and wars for centuries upon centuries. Even when there was surface peace, there was also a seething subterranean element of religious loathing. It would keep my eyes open to possibilities for a United Religions.

Back in New Delhi two incidents enriched my brief stay. First was a visit to the Ramakrishna Ashram. These people had gotten their interfaith inspiration from the greatest interfaith moment in hundreds of years, the moment that the great Swami Vivekananda spoke at the Parliament of World's Religions in Chicago in 1893. He changed the landscape of religion toward a direction of cooperation among faiths. Now, here I was in the ashram of the descendants of Swami Vivekananda, telling Swami Gokulananda about the coming United Religions. Of course he loved it. And we plotted to make it happen. We strategized about extending the invitation to more of the Hindu leaders. Then we walked around the ashram and saw the library, dorms, bookstore, and gardens, then lastly into the Temple where he led me up in front of the chanting congregation while he said his prayers to Ramakrishna.

The second incident was an outdoor press conference attended by reporters from the local Hindu newspaper, a Japanese newspaper, and many others. After I spoke for the ten minutes that I was allotted, there were pledges of support for a United Religions from Baha'i, Hindus, Muslims, and Christians. It was pretty heady stuff. Then a popular figure, Roman Catholic Archbishop Angelo Fernandez, got up to speak. He stood six feet six inches tall, with a mound of mosquitoes elongating his image against the setting sun, so that he appeared to be ten feet tall. Brilliant, saintly, and with a compelling face, he delivered a "stem winder" of a speech for forty-five minutes, drawing upon his vast international interfaith experience. The press conference became his holy filibuster, and he was magnificent. I felt honored to be present.

As he talked, these thoughts flashed through my mind: The reason that religions seem so powerless and impotent in the face of global challenges is because they don't have a common platform from which to speak, from which to take collective action for global good, and from which to hold each other accountable. Someday, young people will look around for help in taking on the problems of the world, and they will notice that religions are content to massage their thoughts of superiority and exclusiveness while avoiding the real matters. They are great at baptisms in water, but silent about the rising waters of climate change. They are great at celebrating life, but quiet about the rising population problem that will suffocate life. The youth will note religion's cowardice in abandoning the needs of the global family in favor of servicing their parochial families of faith. It will take courage, and lots of it, for religions to grow into the new world of faiths together, while at the same time holding on to the ancient roots of fighting faiths. Religion in this [the next] millennium will require the healthiest, most stringent disciplines of the past as well as a willingness to be remade to assist all life in the coming generations. Things will have to be freewheeling for a while, but a look at Christian history teaches us that theology and practice were quite varied at the beginning. It took 300 years for orthodoxy to set in.

What next? Mary and I had seen movies of the Orient Express, so we had built some luxury, we thought, into our trip. We got a first-class compartment to go north to see the Dalai Lama. The inviting picture we had was of the two of us reading in our lovely compartment, then going to the Club Car for a drink and dinner, and then getting into our clean pajamas for a gentle rest before arriving in Pathankot. Well, it wasn't quite like that.

Since the Archbishop had spoken for such a long time, and since we could not just walk away, we left finally in a mad dash for the waiting car that Mary had arranged. The timing was going to be close, but we were anxiously hopeful—until the car broke down in the midst of multiple converging lanes of traffic in a slum area. What to do? We grabbed our two large suitcases and four carry-ons, and jumped into the chaotic street, dodging cars and cows, buses and trucks, all of which were bumping into each other, and we leapt into an empty rickshaw. Clutching all of our luggage to the side of the rickshaw, and getting nudged by nearby vehicles and animals, we started singing, "Nearer My God To Thee." At last we arrived at the station—on time. But we couldn't find our train. We had to step over, or sidestep, thousands of sleeping bodies. Language was a problem. At last we spotted the train. Ah, the waiting luxury!

Sitting in our metallic, sparse, first-class compartment were two men reclining on our beds—bottom beds. Our tickets showed clearly that we were supposed to have the two bottom beds, which we pointed out to them. But this knowledge didn't move them to action. So we stood in our compartment for many miles while they reclined on our beds. Finally they went up top, and we had to calculate about whether or not to take two suitcases and four carry-ons with us to the Club Car, or go to the Club Car one at a time – which would have left Mary alone with these two strangers. We finessed the Club Car, which turned out to be a snack machine. In India "first class" must mean that one person, not you, is in your bed. "Second class" must mean that two people, not you, are in your bed. And "third class" must mean that thirty-three people are in your bed and will eventually eat your bed. I mentioned to Mary that I thought it best to forgo changing into pajamas. So I lay with one eye open all night lest they steal everything. And they, our suite-mates in the top bunks, treated us to a night of muscular and volunteered belching and farting. With only slightly more effort our cabin would have been airborne.

The next day, we awoke to a beautiful sunrise over a verdant, flat terrain that gave way to arid, rocky soil. Tea was served on the train. We arrived an hour late at Pathankot and disembarked alongside a large armed guard delegation for the Punjab Chief Minister, who was also on our train. Tenzin Topgyal, Deputy Secretary of the Tibetan Religion and Culture Department, met us with white scarves. We drove through the very military presence of Sikh soldiers and crossed into Himachal Pradesh to start up the foothills to the mountains. Sleep deprivation dogged us as our car took us up into the Himalayas. Monkeys lined the last part of the highway before Dharamsala.

We climbed past the lower, Hindu town of Dharamsala as we ascended treacherous thin mountain roads up to the Buddhist town of Dharamsala. First we went to the Temple of the Oracle and placed our white scarves there. Then we walked up to the library to see the manuscripts brought from Tibet. This is part of an entire complex of government-in-exile buildings that include Parliament, the Supreme Court, and Security. Maroon-clothed monks and nuns from all over India had gathered for a special religious time. We walked right through the crowd of praying people, who were as indifferent to our intrusion as they would have been to a cow crossing the street. Then we were in front of the Palace of the Dalai Lama.

Before entering the Dalai Lama's Palace we were thoroughly searched. Thoroughly! Evidently the Chinese will occasionally send over a bogus priest or a pretend farmer who will try to kill His Holiness. Someone gave us quick instructions about where we should sit, and sure enough just as the Dalai Lama was about to enter, Mary sat in his seat. Instantly, a correction was made.

I was oh so grateful to friends Senator Dianne Feinstein and her husband Richard Blum for arranging this appointment. So, I started by bringing their greetings. Then we got quickly and deeply into the vision of a United Religions. His Holiness got it. The prospect of unity was his big take-away. For instance, he cited the divisions among the Greek Orthodox, especially between the Patriarch in Istanbul and the Patriarch in Russia. The Dalai Lama said that instead of weeping over the inability to find organic unity, why not find another way of finding unity, through a United Religions? He thought that through accentuating unity we could focus on the best of our past traditions and in addition we could, in the future, take meaningful social actions together around the world. Over and over again he said, "I support the vision." Also, he encouraged me to teach that UR will not be a once-in-a-while conference with many people speaking to a large audience, but instead will be about people of different faiths taking on action projects together.

I gave the Dalai Lama a tray with the seal of the Diocese of California and a picture of himself. It depicts His Holiness in the University of California Golden Bears colors, blue and gold. He picked it out immediately. We took lots of pictures, he presented us with white scarves, and then he held our hands and the three of us were quiet and prayerful for a long moment. Then we were gone. I could not have felt better.

We went to dinner at the Institute at bottom of the mountain, and then drove up the mountain again, this time after dark, so no one was on the road. Despite that fact, it had to be the worst drive of my life on a road that mostly isn't a road with one lane that frequently shrinks to less. Corners call for going forward halfway and backing up, or else making the whole turn in one effort by squeezing around sheer rock. Thousands of feet drop beside your tires, which are inches from the edge. When monks, cows, or tourists are sharing the road, the driver speeds up while honking the horn madly. When buses or trucks come the other way, it is prayer time. Anyway, we climbed into our cold bed in a cold room later than we had wanted.

For the second night in a row we slept in our clothes in order to be ready for a 4:30 a.m. wake up call. We were told to leave early because the Buddhist car often broke down. And, what a ride: we saw one dead monkey, one wrecked car, one dead horse, one head-on collision of buses—did I mention that the roads coming off the mountain were narrow?—and as we approached Jammu-Kashmir, one dead person in the road. Sixteen persons had died along this road yesterday in clashes between the Hindu Kashmiris and the Muslim Kashmiris. The tension from this conflict mounted the closer we got to the airport. We were searched four times and our passports were taken away from us.

After a long wait, we got on a plane to Mumbai at night. In Mumbai, completely exhausted, we took a cab to the Ramada Hotel, where we found that we had no reservations. Patience was thin and prospects of finding a room in that filled-up town at a late hour were thinner. Eventually ("eventually" means tipping sixteen more people who grab our luggage, salute and ask for a tip), we landed in a decent little hotel.

Mary was phenomenal in arranging flights and lodging and appointments and transportation in foreign countries while we were almost frantically on the move. She did it by way of difficult telephone calls, and with a computer—trying to get to people who had no computers. And she came through every time for the whole intense, three-month journey.

In the end, almost everything turned upside down. Despite the Dalai Lama's initial excitement about a United Religions, he would have nothing to do with the URI in the long run. Despite my interacting exclusively with the elite of Pakistan, the URI took root there among grassroots people, and seventeen years later, Pakistan is in the top three countries of the world with URI Cooperation Circles. The most encouraging religious leader in India, in responding to the idea of a United Religions, was dead one month after our conversation. The Orient Express trip turned out to be a joke. Nevertheless, whatever momentum there was seemed to reside in the miscellaneous, unplanned conversations. I was learning that there are decisive dimensions at play in a grand pursuit, and these dimensions are not at all recognizable at the time. There is more going on than meets the eye or penetrates the brain. But at that moment I was leaving India absolutely clueless as to the efficacy of my pilgrimage. I was thrilled by the privilege of the encounters but ambiguous as to whether or not I was on to something big.

Chapter 10
The Great Journey—Dashed Hopes and Hopeful Serendipity

When our work in India was complete we headed for Mauritius, an island nation in the Indian Ocean about 1,200 miles off the southeast coast of the African continent, for ten days of rest and relaxation. Arriving at the International Terminal at 4:30 a.m., we endured a long hassle over the weight of our luggage (it cost us $90 extra). Feeling completely numb and having worn the same clothes for three straight days, we embarked on what turned out to be our second fantasy of luxury.

Like our dashed high hopes for a luxurious trip on the Orient Express, Mauritius also proved to be an adventure in dashed hopes. Upon arrival I came down with a high temperature and a respiratory infection that lasted for weeks. My eyes turned red, and got even redder when a truck backfired in my face. To add to the dismal mood, we received emails from San Francisco informing us that five foundations had turned us down for grants to next year's Charter Writing Session, and one of our most promising sponsors of that event had backed out.

We finally got off the island and back to Mumbai where I was to give a talk to a small gathering of religious leaders, and things just got worse. For the talk, I tried out the important speech I was to give in Oxford in a few weeks. Then on our way back to our hotel in a cab, to my horror, the pages of the talk came undone and scattered all over the floor of the cab. The driver insisted that he would get them together and return soon to take us to the airport for our trip to Cairo. Of course when the time came, our driver never showed up. We waited until our flight departure time was in jeopardy and stormed off to the airport. Yes, it was our only copy of the Oxford talk. Sick, discouraged, and panicked, I arrived in Cairo with no appointments scheduled and no one to help along the way. All we had was a hotel reservation for four days. Of course when we arrived at the hotel, the manager insisted that we could only stay for two. Perfect! What now?

Because it was Sunday, we went to church, which happened to be at a beautiful new cathedral. Although the Episcopal Bishop of Egypt, Ghais Malik, was supposed to be around his diocese on that Sunday, he unexpectedly showed up at his cathedral, All Saints. Since I had worked with him at the 1988 Lambeth Conference in Canterbury, England, we fell on each others' shoulders like long-lost brothers. He asked what I was doing in Cairo, and I said that although I had been unsuccessful in arranging an appointment with the Sheik of al-Azhar (a high authority on Sunni Islamic thought), I came hoping against hope for an appointment at the last minute. Ghais grabbed my arm. After a long silence he said, "He died two days ago."

Actually, this sad moment was the beginning of a series of unexpected positive circumstances. The first was that I tagged along, the next day, with the bishop as he went for a doctor's appointment. The doctor saw me as well, and soon afterwards my newly diagnosed viral flu began to abate. And then, by exercising computer magic, Mary was able to retrieve my Oxford talk—and thus a great weight fell from my shoulders.

During all of these travels I was writing like mad. I was writing articles for the San Jose Mercury News, I was writing a diary every night on the activities of the day before going to sleep, and I was working on sermons and talks. I was also researching, as best I could, information about the people I was going to meet with, to prepare for my appointments. Having a little breathing room in Cairo and feeling healthier every day helped my energy levels.

Bishop Malik had arranged for me to have an appointment with the Grand Mufti of Egypt, Dr. Mohammed Sayed Tantawi on Wednesday, March 20. A Grand Mufti is the highest official of religious law in Sunni Islam. His opinions reverberate around the world. He worked in Cairo in a building named Dar El Eftaa, which means, "a house of answering questions." He has official status in the government in that he is affiliated with the Ministry of Judges. Thank goodness we arrived early because the Grand Mufti had just received word from the office of President Hosni Mubarak that his presence was needed quickly in the president's office. Little did I know that the president was going to appoint him to be the next Sheik of al-Azhar. Unbeknownst to me, I actually was going to see the Sheik of al-Azhar after all.

The Grand Mufti was a man of medium build in a black robe, with a white round hat that was topped in scarlet. He was a gentle man who said "thank you" continuously. After hearing about the coming United Religions, he said that when the light of one religion burns, it is a great blessing, but that when the lights of many religions burn at the same time, it will be radiant and bring abundant blessings. He advised me to present the vision "gently." He said that he would be honored to participate in the Charter Writing Session, either personally or through a delegation. We drank tea; he walked me to the elevator and wished me God's blessings. He seemed to be a man carrying a great weight of responsibility, was of a quiet nature, and had bashful, probing eyes. We parted company and he went off the meet with the president who would appoint him to be the next Sheik of al-Azhar.

I could have flown away from Cairo that moment and been far, far ahead of the game. But one more unlikely treat was in store: an appointment with the Pope of the Coptic Church, His Holiness, Shenouda III. Inside the Coptic compound in Cairo there is an ancient cathedral and the offices of the Pope. What a man! Seventy-two years old, a former president of the World Council of Churches, he loved pontificating in conversations, appeared to be highly energetic, had a sense of humor, and always insisted that the dialogue go deeper. Talking with him was a real workout, but wonderfully worth it. He kept referring to the United Religions as "a conference," stating that we would have to get beyond that. Also, he continued the theme of other religious leaders that we would be charged with promoting "synchronisms," blending all religions into one bowl of tasteless porridge. And like the Shankaracharya and the Dalai Lama, he giggled at moments of profound truth. When I mentioned early on that the United Religions intended to change the world, he said that not even God could do that. To which I said that the world was going to change anyway and the issue was whether or not religion would be on the side of God's unfolding will and the good, or whether religion would be bogged down, merely protecting its past revelations from God. At his most extravagant praise, he thought that the United Religions was at least aimed in a God-ward direction. As for the Charter Writing Session planned for next year, he wouldn't have the Coptic Church venture that far out, but he was glad to be alerted, and promised to keep an open mind. Years later, when he died in the middle of the Arab Spring of 2012 and the persecution of Coptic Christians, I often thought back on that remarkable man. And I was glad that many Coptic Christians aligned with the eventual United Religions Initiative and found great hope in solidarity during times of terror.

Two more highlights of the conversation: First, he gave a long soliloquy on Jonah aboard the ship that was about to sink. The Captain asked people of all religions on the ship to pray to their Deity for deliverance. And the prayers of all the people were answered. Second, he talked about the Communist times in Russia when the Government tried to wipe out the religious faith of the people. He said that mothers and grand-mothers told their children and grandchildren stories of their faith, and that is what kept the faith alive for the entire seventy-five years of atheism. He said it was like the story of Moses and his mother. Although Moses was raised in the household of Pharaoh amidst the worship of Pharaonic gods and goddesses, he kept hearing the stories of Hebrew faith that his mother never gave up telling. I had no idea what this latter story had to do with the blessings of interfaith, but it seemed insightful to me at the level of how to sustain one's own faith during times of persecution or hardship. At the end of the meeting, he gave us medals of the Holy Family in Egypt, and gave Mary a cross.

So, out of Egypt Mary and I flew, restored and invigorated. We had twelve days until my Oxford talk, so we were open to explore possibilities. The next stop became obvious because we were in the neighborhood. We flew next door to Israel, even though we had no appointments lined up. We had worked off and on for eight years in a Companion Relationship between the Episcopal Diocese of Jerusalem and the Episcopal Diocese of California, and thus had spent quality time in Gaza, the West Bank, and Israel, so we were confident that our many relationships could be mined. Chief among these friendships was the one with Rabbi David Rosen.

On the first day in Jerusalem I successfully arranged a meeting with Rabbi Mordechai Piron, Head of the Spiritual Center of Culture and Education. He had been an army chaplain for fifty years and eventually became the Chief Rabbi of the Army. After a deeply engaging exchange, a light bulb went off over his head. He said, "You know, this United Religions could end up being bigger than you and I could imagine. It is inevitable; it has to happen." Our wide-ranging conversation then covered everything from where Mary could go to shop for gold jewelry, to a press conference, to Trinitarian theology. Rabbi Piron was a God-sent ally to me.

News came from San Francisco that the wife of my dear friend Richard Goldman had died, so I went to the Western Wall, donned a white skull cap, wrote a prayer for Rhoda, placed my head against the wall, and prayed. Then I walked through nearly empty streets to the Holy Sepulcher of the Christians and prayed. A suicide bomber had killed many people the previous day in a tragic bus explosion. That explained why there were so few people venturing out on the streets that day.

On very short notice the Episcopal Bishop of Jerusalem, Samir Kafity, gathered a colorful group of guests for a celebrative dinner in honor of Mary's birthday, March 21, the first day of spring. We shared high spirits, good laughs, and cherished memories—and the bishop got genuinely excited about the prospect of a United Religions. He then instructed his Administrative Officer to set up an appointment for us with Crown Prince Hassan of Jordan two days thence, and to make all of the necessary plans. What mind-boggling Middle-Eastern hospitality!

A rabbi friend of mine in San Francisco had advised me to get in touch with the Executive Director of the World Union of Progressive Judaism, Rabbi Richard Hirsch. So the next morning I sat down with Rabbi Hirsch, who hurried through our conversation and seemed mentally occupied elsewhere. Finally, he talked about working with Martin Luther King, Jr., and other civil rights workers in America; although they had worked together, it seems that the U.S. civil rights workers were unresponsive in offering help to Israel after the Six-Day War in 1967. So he was cynical about people of great religions coming together to do anything. Yet the vision of a United Religions finally took root in him, and he became genuinely excited, especially about the prospect of it being headquartered in the Presidio of San Francisco. He wanted me to meet Rabbi Hugo Gryn in London, which, in time, actually happened.

Next day we went over the famous Allenby Bridge, which laughably is two bus-lengths long. But a very important two bus-lengths because it both connects and separates Jordan and Israel. We journeyed to Mt. Nebo, the place that Moses died before entering the "Promised Land." Another highlight was interviewing Dr. Raouf Sa'd Abu Jaber, Chairman of the Orthodox Central Committee. He was born in nearby Salt, Jordan, and earned a Doctorate in History at Oxford. His experience is in Christian-Muslim dialogue. So by the end of the day, although I felt quite sick (a carry-over from India) and exhausted, we were ensconced in a place we had only dreamed about, the place where Moses died.

On the negative side, I never did get to meet Crown Prince Hassan of Jordan. I was told that the King was out of the country, and since the Crown Prince was in charge of state matters, he simply didn't have time to see me. But I did have an energetic meeting with two members of the Board of the Royal Institute for Interfaith Studies—at the time, the only Islamic interfaith institute in the world. They worried about the Pope's reaction to my initiative, as did I. In so many places I visited in the world, religious leaders wondered first of all what the Pope would think of a United Religions. Clearly, no one wanted to be on his bad side in this matter. So I left them a copy of my Oxford talk and Mary and I went off to meet some interesting old Christian leaders.

One of them was Bishop Khoury who had served on the Board of the Palestine Liberation Organization. As might be imagined, he spent time in jail—two months. In that time he read the Bible eleven times and memorized 200 hymns. His lawyer quipped, "You read the Bible eleven times? Let's throw all of the priests in jail!"

The wife of Fai'k Haddad, a former bishop in Jerusalem, told me that years ago, she was serving on the altar in the cathedral in Jerusalem, and after the service she noticed a frazzled, bedraggled man wandering around in the back of the church. She went back to see if she could help him, and he turned out to be Bishop James Albert Pike, fifth Bishop of the Episcopal Diocese of California (I am the seventh). They chatted and joked about him coming to dinner. Then two days later he was found dead in the Judean Desert.

I had many conversations with the man assigned by the Episcopal Church in Jordan to take us around Amman. I mentioned how impressed I was with Israeli young people, hundreds of them in Jerusalem, who had held a peace rally even in the face of the suicide bombing. I asked if anything like that would ever happen among the Arab youth. He said, "No, they have too much long-term hostility after being chased from their farms, imprisoned, and tortured. They are not keen on peace with Israel. As a matter of fact 'peace' is not a positive word among them." Then we went back over the little Allenby Bridge to the other side of the argument.

The next day I walked around a rainy Jerusalem looking for the office of Rabbi David Rosen, who had been recommended to me in the highest terms. It was surprising that he was in, and he took time to drop everything and talk with me. David was once the Chief Rabbi of Ireland, and when we met, he was President of the World Conference of Religion and Peace as well as being the head of the Anti-Defamation League. The previous year (1995) he had been invited to the prestigious World Economic Forum in Davos, Switzerland. Invitees were always world leaders, prime ministers, and Fortune 500 types, so to have a religious leader invited was quite extraordinary. After a little while of talking with him, I was sure that his invitation was well deserved.

He gave me the telephone number of the head of the World Economic Forum, Klaus Schwabe, who at the previous year's session had publicly stated that there should be a United Nations of Religions. He strongly urged me to go quickly to Geneva and follow up on that remark. He also encouraged me to visit with Konrad Raiser, the Secretary General of the World Council of Churches while in Geneva. When I got back to our room, Mary dove right in to finding time on our schedule, and looking into airplane and hotel reservations.

Meanwhile, Rabbi Rosen gave me a briefing on the hierarchy of the Vatican and whom I should definitely meet if I could. Then he gave me a briefing on the "modern" and "old European" tensions within Judaism and how each side would respond to interfaith possibilities. Then, after asking probing questions about the coming United Religions, we drew a map of the world of Judaism, and Rabbi Rosen explained how many people from each nation and religious strand should be invited to the Charter Writing Session. Not only had I hit a gold mine of important information and contacts, I had made a friend for life. Two days later, two telephone calls came from Geneva, and I had appointments at the World Economic Forum and the World Council of Churches on April 18, less than a month away. The surprises just kept coming.

Later that day, I stopped in at the brand new offices of the Mayor of Jerusalem, Ehud Olmert. I brought greetings from friends of his in San Francisco, and told him about the coming United Religions. His reaction was positive, and he especially liked the idea of it being headquartered in the Presidio of San Francisco.

Looking back on this part of the journey, it is clear that I was learning a lot, making friends, and planting seeds. In truth, the seeds eventually sprouted up in fields that I could not have envisaged at the time. In Egypt, when the Arab Spring burst forth in 2010, URI had everything to do with ordinary people, and nothing to do with the religious establishment. In Jordan, the Royal Institute for International Studies would have nothing to do with me—and continued to have nothing to do with me when I returned nine years later with a the Global Council and staff of URI. And in Geneva, URI turned out to make not a blip on the screen of the World Council of Churches or the World Economic Forum. Nevertheless, every one of them offered me crucial insights, and filled out a large canvas of religious reality, which I needed to observe and critique.

Chapter 11
The Great Journey—
Will It Fly With My People?

As an Episcopal bishop, and thus an integral part of the Anglican Communion, the day had to come when I would "go
home" and find out what my own people thought of me
and my idea. What better places than at Oxford University
and Lambeth Palace, London, the office of the Archbishop
of Canterbury, head of the international Anglican Communion. What better audience than an Anglican interfaith gathering and quality time with the Archbishop of Canterbury,
George Carey? If I could make it there, perhaps I could
make it anywhere. But then again, if I bombed in Oxford
and London, what chance would I have of succeeding elsewhere? Is this prophet going to be without honor in his own
country? Therefore, a great deal was riding on the next few
days, as Mary and I boarded the plane to fly from the Middle East to London.

On a beautiful day in late March, Mary and I found ourselves
driving through an English countryside, with green fields,
daffodils, and forsythia—and arriving at a 17th century farm-
house, named Pin Farm, the home of Celia and David Storey,
near Oxford. Whew! The big interfaith conference was five
days away, and we were trying to orient ourselves to the place
and the people and issues that were floating around.

One of the other guests staying at Pin Farm was a young German theological student named Josef Boehle. He strongly
suggested that we fly to Tubingen, Germany, and speak with
the famous professor of theology, Hans Kung. It was a good
idea but I didn't know Hans Kung, didn't know if he would
see me, and didn't know if we had time to squeeze in a trip

to Germany. In a flash, Josef called the professor, Mary made the arrangements, and Tubingen was now on our itinerary.

The interfaith conference was championed by the various interfaith bodies that swirled around Oxford and tended to work well together. There was the Rev. Marcus Braybrooke of the International Interfaith Centre; David and Celia Storey of the World Congress of Faiths; and Dr. Robert Traer of the International Association for Religious Freedom. Always in the mix on such occasions was the World Conference for Religion and Peace. It took a while for us just to get the lay of the land. It took only a second to figure out who was sympathetic to the coming United Religions and who opposed it with vigor. My speech was going to be a workout.

On April 2, 1996 came my big talk at Oxford in front of several hundred people. There was a lot wrong with it. For instance, I started much too slowly and pedantically. My delivery was uneven. I described a half-baked suggestion for organizational design. And the whole talk lasted much too long. I even had to scrap a third of my talk and just summarize it in a hurry to the audience. On the other hand, in my opinion, I had made several legitimate points, including saying, "The great religions can either operate in the responsibility of interaction or in the isolation of denial of having a global vocation." I thought that delineating my reasons why a United Religions should exist was my strongest argument. Among the nine reasons that I mentioned was this one: "Because someday, the ascendancy of militant fundamentalist voices of politically aspiring religions might be so pervasive that a United Religions will need to be created in order to save the religions from their ethnic, tribal agendas."

This is how I ended the Oxford speech:

"For there to be a United Religions in the future, several things have to happen. First and foremost, the imagination of grass-roots people has to be set ablaze, so that they pray and advocate for its birth. Local interfaith councils and campus interfaith groups must call for a United Religions using publicity and the Internet. If the grassroots do not get the vision, there will not be an authentic United Religions.

"Second, the established international interfaith groups have to give it their genuine, wholehearted support. They are the ones who have borne the burden in the heat of the day. Whatever interfaith network that exists today is there because of their labors. If they do not agree that a United Religions is needed and that a United Religions would ultimately benefit their ministry, then a United Religions will not happen.

"Third, the great religions of the world have never been asked to come together on a daily basis, like the United Nations, to address global good. This is, by far, the most ambitious challenge ever put before them regarding sharing authority for global good. If they back away, a United Religions will not happen.

"Personally I am optimistic about the United Religions. It will happen because it has to happen. The predictability of all factors coming together is improbable. But humanity has always stretched to find its soul in new and foreign settings. The reason that religions are so impotent today, in the face of this brand new emerging global civilization, is that religions have shrunk from the challenge of discovering a common voice, a global voice. Young people know this in their deepest being. They are moving into this global civilization with all of its con-traditions and challenges, realizing the cowardice and quiet of the religions in their abandonment of the global family in favor of the exclusivity of parochial families. Religions gave birth to a world they then orphaned when the world grew up. They have become deadbeat fathers and mothers while their modern children walk around trying to piece together enough religion to make decisions about the future. They add a little yoga to the words of the Prophet, a little Catechism to a little Dharma. They will find their way eventually because humanity has always stretched to find its soul in new and foreign settings. One way or another, in Bangalore or in your grandchild, a United Religions will happen."

The audience by and large disapproved of my whole speech. Most of the vociferous points of contention centered on starting from the top down: organizing with "recognizable historic religious traditions" instead of organizing with the grassroots. Also, this group did not want anything to do with a United Religions that operated with a bureaucracy. So the question and answer session immediately turned into a rant by the audience, which was followed by boos. Before leaving the stage, I acknowledged that they were not impressed. Nevertheless, I promised that I would stick with it, regardless of their reaction, until someday there would be a United Religions. Some people who disagreed with my paper appreciated my resolve and said they would join me on my quest.

In the long haul, the audience was right. It would take a while for me to incorporate their specific criticisms. Nevertheless, I was onto something. And I knew it. I was just in over my head. I didn't lack for courage or broad insight. I lacked in total grasp of what was needed to make it real. It began to dawn on me that this was not the time for a United Religions, not the fullness of time for that vision. But it was time for something along those lines, and I was determined to keep hewing at the rock until it broke open.

Someone made a statement that I didn't want to lose. The person said that the Charter of the United Nations begins with the words, "We the People." But the U.N. isn't the people; it is the place where sovereign nations vie for their own self-interest. If there is ever a United Religions and it starts with the words, "We the People," it really has to be about the peoples of faiths and not the self interests of competing religions.

Two days after April Fool's Day in 1996, I was reeling. I still had my solid vision but two large cracks had appeared in it. Yes, in India, Cairo, and Jerusalem, religious leaders had responded favorably to my United Religions vision and urged me to stay on course with my plan for a Charter Writing Session. But from San Francisco, hadn't I received news that the money for the Charter Writing Session was not going to be there? And in Oxford, hadn't the crowd let me know that I was starting at the wrong end; that I should begin with grassroots and not with the people at the top of religion? And that it should more of an organism than an organization?

Yet even in Oxford, some people got my message. Marcus Braybrooke followed up by writing a paragraph for publication describing how the United Religions would be more important than present international interfaith organizations. Surprisingly, a board member of the world's largest international interfaith organization, World Conference for Religion and Peace, got it. She saw that a United Religions would be a symbolic place that sends a message that religions do belong to each other at their center. It would be a forum for religions to discover their common voice in speaking together to the world's crucial issues, and taking actions together. Such comments fed my stubbornness, so even though I was smarting from the reaction in Oxford, I was ready to carry on with the vision.

Our lives took a distinctly Anglican turn at this point of the journey. Principal to this part of our journey was an appointment with the Archbishop of Canterbury, George Carey. Although I had written a year in advance for an appointment, his office always wrote back saying that he would be out of town during the weeks when I was to be in England. But the newspapers each day showed that he was very much in town. Here I was on a journey where I could meet almost every great religious leader on earth, eventually including Pope John Paul II, and the one who blatantly refused to see me was my own Archbishop of Canterbury. Why? I didn't know. But I was livid. Hadn't he asked me, personally, to raise $500,000 so he could offer bishops from poor dioceses scholarships to attend the 1998 Lambeth Conference? And hadn't I come through for him? I never received a "thank you." And now, I couldn't get even an appointment. I wrote a scathing letter to the Archbishop, which Mary threw away. Then I wrote him an angry letter, which Mary threw away. Finally I wrote a courteous letter that got by my bedroom censor, and its reply granted me an appointment at Lambeth Palace with someone on his staff who turned out to be the Rev. Andrew Deuchar. The time with him went wonderfully well, and he said that he thought that the United Religions was a worthy topic and he would try to arrange an appointment with the Archbishop for a couple of weeks thence.

I need to say a word here about Marcus Braybrooke, who was, in my opinion, the global dean of international interfaith work. It was he who joined me in New York on June 21, 1993 and suggested that I launch my vision with a youth event before the U.N. 50th celebration. It was Marcus who came to all of our early events. It was Marcus who made sure that I was invited to this Oxford Interfaith Conference. And on Palm Sunday, March 31, 1996, it was Marcus who invited me to preach in his two rural churches at Toot Baldon and Marsh Baldon, Oxfordshire. It was Marcus and Mary Braybrooke who hosted a dinner for us, and ended it with English Stilton cheese. Such cheese she would smuggle to me in various places around the world when we would have reunions. But on Palm Sunday, after hymns and prayers in church, the entire congregation, carrying palm branches, walked through lanes, across England's largest Green, stopping at houses and pubs for prayers, and ended up at St. Peter's Church, Marsh Baldon for Holy Eucharist.

The walk was very cold and damp underfoot, but a marvelous experience. Afterwards, a warden of the church gave us a tour of the manor house of this area with its garden, barns and fields. And then we went briefly for tea at the rectory of Mary and Marcus Braybrooke. We went for lunch to the Global Retreat House run by the Brahma Kumaris, a Hindu offshoot. What an estate, with an immaculate, well-appointed mansion atop a hill overlooking vast lands with the Thames River running along at the bottom.

On Maundy Thursday, Richard Harries, the Bishop of Oxford and an old friend from Lambeth 1988, invited me to vest for the "Chrism Mass" at Christ Church College. On Good Friday, I delivered two meditations at St. Peter's, Marsh Baldon. Earlier, Mary and I had visited with the Bishop of London, Richard Chartres, an old friend from his 1981 visit to San Francisco. He took us to the House of Lords, where he is a member, and we had lunch with him there.

On this Good Friday an invitation arrived saying that I had been nominated for Presiding Bishop, and asking if I would be a candidate. It was not good for digestion at dinner because I did not want to take up discerning a call to take on the top job of the Episcopal Church while I was so engrossed in my quest to start a United Religions.

Then, at the Easter Vigil at St. Paul's Cathedral, Bishop Chartres began his sermon by shouting, "Alleluia, Christ is Risen!" to which the congregation gave a timid response of "He is risen, indeed. Alleluia." Bishop Chartres then said, "Mercy, mercy, that is so weak. Here I am with the Bishop of California watching our feeble display of enthusiasm. Come on now, let's try it again." On Easter Sunday I participated in the great service at St. Paul's Cathedral where thousands attended. When I wondered out loud about who all of these people were, Bishop Chartres said, "Cathedrals have advantages over parishes because so many individuals want anonymity and aren't prepared for the full frontal intimacy of a parish church."

For the next couple of days we toured and relaxed. We went to see the seventh century Dorchester Abbey. We visited a house built outside Oxford in 1538 where the students could go to escape the sixteenth century plague. We chatted with the faculty at Cuddesdon Theological College where several friends, including Desmond Tutu, had attended. I even played a round of golf in the little village of Nettlebed. This village's most famous citizens were actor Jeremy Irons and author Ian Fleming, who wrote the James Bond books.

Being in England was, in many instances, luxurious, in that I was in my theological and ethnic comfort zone, and I had a golden opportunity to participate in the events of Holy Week away from the demands of being a diocesan bishop. I could just worship and didn't have to lead worship services. Yes, I had some bruises and bumps from this time in England, but I figured that the encounters made me stronger and better prepared for the tests ahead on the quest. I knew that I would be returning to London soon for a brief session with the Archbishop of Canterbury, so there was an unfinished feeling as Mary and I drove to Heathrow airport past hilltops white with snow.

Chapter 12
The Great Journey — Hard Realities

Earlier in San Francisco, we had two dear friends who not only encouraged us to visit the Ecumenical Patriarch, His All Holiness, Bartholomew, in Istanbul, but they personally wrote to him to arrange an audience. One was a famous Greek Orthodox layman, George Marcus, and the other was Metropolitan Anthony of the Orthodox Church of the West. We were assured of a warm welcome, and that is exactly what we received. Interestingly, Orthodox Church of the East, which operates from a different calendar than the Church in the West, was about to celebrate Easter on the morning after our Saturday arrival in Istanbul. So we had two authentic Easters in eight days.

We woke up early on Easter and headed for the Patriarchate and the Cathedral of St. George. At the end of the long, deep, musically-rich service, everyone went forward to receive a red Easter egg, as a symbol of new life. When we got back to the hotel, Mary stayed out in the hallway while I hid the two eggs in our hotel room. Then we switched and I stayed in the hallway while she hid the eggs. It wasn't a traditional Easter egg hunt, but it would do in a pinch.

I had met Patriarch Bartholomew on several occasions in San Francisco and admired him greatly. On Tuesday, while bishops from all over the world were milling around, he had a special audience for Mary and me. His office had one large icon, a 200-year-old embroidered picture of a young Jesus bearing a cross, five elegant candelabras, and flowers everywhere, a carryover from Easter. We discussed the United Religions. The topic caught him off guard, and it took five years for us to have an opportunity to engage in an in-depth discussion. Meanwhile, it was time for the great luncheon feast for all of the dignitaries. An aide was assigned to me to help me address the dignitaries properly. As someone approached, he would whisper in my ear, "Your Beatitude," or, "Your Excellency." But in reality, when a surly, sinister-looking prelate approached, my aide whispered, "Your Bad Attitude." Or when a large bishop approached, he whispered, "Your Amplitude." The naughty archimandrite kept the day light for me.

For Mary, there were several dimensions to this visit. Prior to our arrival, the Patriarch had mentioned in a letter to me how much he was looking forward to meeting "Her Excellency, Mrs. Swing." So she, Mary Taylor Swing, went out and ordered bath towels that were monogrammed with "HE—MTS." On the big day, since women are not permitted to dine with the men, she went downstairs and had lunch with four women and a deacon who apologized for not being in the twentieth century. But it was all good. How could we not love the Greek Orthodox?

Almost like magic, one day later, on April 17, 1996, we walked across a bridge over the Rhone River, just where it leaves Lake Geneva and before it merges with the Arve River. Stunningly beautiful Geneva! Then we took a cab to the headquarters of the World Council of Churches. The General Secretary, Dr. Konrad Raiser, was out of town, but I had the extreme privilege of spending a few hours with two of the most knowledgeable interfaith experts that I had encountered, namely the Rev. Dr. Wesley Ariarajah, Deputy General Secretary in the Office on Inter-Religious Relations, and the Rev. Hans Ucko of that staff.

Clearly, the core of the World Council of Churches work was with Christians, but inevitably, the interfaith dimension has come into their focus. Two new areas of study and emphasis for them have been interfaith work and Muslim-Christian dialogue, especially around the hard issues of the political goals of these two religions. Clearly they were light-years ahead of me in knowing what they were talking about in terms of religions dealing with each other.

For instance, how does a typical believer of one faith learn about other faiths? Their answer: through the media and through the way one's own tradition teaches about other faiths. Every day, throughout the world, interfaith education is undertaken by newspapers, radios and television, which keep up a steady stream of interfaith teaching about other religions—and usually from an obtuse angle. Consequently, a deep stereotype lurks in a national or regional populace regarding "foreign" religions. Moreover, one's own local religion would not dare to be fair and reasonable about other religions, for fear of losing people to other faiths, and for fear of a backlash. So the real teachers of interfaith hardly ever rise above propaganda, and the world is severely handicapped in addressing issues that are so tied into religions.

Another for instance: What is the best possible way for interfaith to be learned? Their answer: away from home base, in hard dialogue, in serious study and sharing. But that must be done in a context of granted immunity from customary religious bias, and a long-term commitment to interfaith learning. If the learner only stays at home base, listening to the media and only to one's own religious teacher talk about other faiths, little new information will be learned. Only when the learner gets away from uniform interfaith teaching and engages real people of other faiths, confronts real differences, builds new alliances of respect, and takes on mutual responsibility for addressing mutual problems, only then will the learner become an interfaith presence for reconciliation. They said that, "We have grown up in a century of interfaith opinion. We aspire to create a century of interfaith work."

I can still hear them appealing to me that a United Religions should not start out to be a problem-solving organization, but should initially be about securing a long-term commitment to be the context in which problems can be solved. Also, here we were in Europe, where scholarly theology is a main staple of religion, so it follows that ministry starts with learning and leads to action. My fear at this point was that everyone would have to earn a Ph.D. before we got started. Being a pragmatic American, I think in terms of action that leads to learning. Obviously, it has to be "both/and." In a United Religions, all participants would have to understand through learning and action, and would have to practice their own faiths in the context of all faiths, for the sake of life on this planet.

These two men asked me all of the classic questions about a United Religions—about representation, money, turf, and more—but mostly they were looking to see if I were just another harebrained, naïve do-gooder, or if United Religions had any substance and hard thought behind it. I took my best shot. They didn't seem overwhelmed by me or what I was saying, but they were, at least, respectful.

One bit of advice to me was not to place much emphasis on religious celebrities. Up to then, interfaith conferences lived or died on the participation of religious celebrities who, by their presence, conferred legitimacy and merit on the gathering. But with celebrities come problems. They fly in, give a speech (which is or is not on the point of the conference) and walk away without taking on the burden of what the conference is all about. And just because the religious celebrity appeared and spoke, it didn't mean that his or her official religious body backed the conference.

I had lots of lessons to learn, and suggestions to be digested. I was supremely grateful to these two men who were way ahead of me in interfaith knowledge, and who took the time to give me their insights.

Geneva turned out to be a bonanza for me, even though I had never imagined that it would—or even that I would be there. On a glorious Thursday, with the Swiss Alps to the East and the French Alps to the West, and with tulips, pansies, forsythia, and fruit trees popping into bloom, we drove up a verdant hillside to Cologny, the most luxurious neighborhood of Geneva, to meet David Morrison and Alexander McLin of the World Economic Forum.

Interestingly enough, these two hard-working, humble professionals had just returned from the U.S., where they had interviewed people at various think tanks. Dealing with political, economic and scientific thinkers in all of their recent travels, one theme emerged universally—people kept speculating out loud that there is a spiritual deficiency at the heart of capitalism, and that the void was beginning to touch all aspects of life. They predicted that people the world over would be turning toward a religious or spiritual direction in the next decades, to make up for what capitalism doesn't touch. After an overdose of secularism, the world will now swing in a direction of "de-secularization." Since these men were predicting that religion would play a much greater role in shaping the world in the next period of time, they were fascinated to hear about a United Religions. They were genuinely interested and wanted to be kept in the loop of our progress. They wondered why efforts to create a United Religions had failed in the past, but that did not stop them from imagining that their work and mine would be overlapping.

Through the magic of Mary and our travel agent at "Above and Beyond" in San Francisco, we were walking that evening through the streets of Tubingen, Germany. It was the first night of spring weather, and so the students at the University of Tubingen flocked to the pubs and restaurants. After crossing the Neckar River, we walked uphill into a breathtaking view of the old city of half-timbered buildings and plazas set around a dominating cathedral, and we joined the students. The atmosphere was intoxicating. We picked a very German restaurant and couldn't read the menu. Nevertheless, by exhausting the thin shred of compassion of our waitress, we ordered an excellent meal. But some of the night's magic faded when the waitress wouldn't accept our Visa card or Travelers Checks. So I took a rare ATM tour of Tubingen, leaving Mary as hostage back in the restaurant with a mound of spaetzle.

My journey was coming to an end—and now for the main event! I was keenly aware when I woke up in Tubingen on April 19, 1996, of the importance of the next seven days. I would be speaking with the most prolific, most popular theologian of the twentieth century, Professor Dr. Hans Kung. I would be speaking with the president of the Pontifical Council for Interreligious Dialogue in the Vatican in Rome. And I would be speaking with the Archbishop of Canterbury at Lambeth Palace in London. If I were ever going to have a hand in creating a United Religions, I would have to pass the test in these three interviews. So the stakes were high.

Hans Kung was approachable and unhurried, and obviously he had read my Oxford talk with great thoroughness. The next two hours mentally exhausted me as Hans Kung addressed one subject after another in systematic precision and in rapid fire. He quickly dismissed the idea of using buildings in the Presidio, saying that it would be cumbersome to begin with a bureaucracy, especially when it would not be the central issue. The central issue was to work toward the consent of the religions and the creation of a Charter. That might have to come in stages. The first stage could last for ten years, according to Kung, while distinguished religious leaders from each tradition (supported by staffs) would keep up the dialogue on the creation of a United Religions. At the end of ten years, the religions themselves would create and carry out a United Religions.

The clear impression that I received from Hans Kung was that I, personally, would have to make a crucial decision for myself. Either I was to pursue the great religious leaders ("celebrities") and try to create something with them, or I was to aim at the world's six billion people and try to create something with them. He cautioned that the religious celebrities were unreliable and fickle, while the six billion would be unmanageable and chaotic. Nevertheless, I shouldn't sail off in two directions but settle on one and then stay with it.

In an easier moment in the conversations that progressed from his living room to his porch, and from his porch to his front yard, Hans Kung talked about his involvement in his Roman Catholic parish church in Switzerland and how, as a priest, he still celebrated the sacraments there. As we were saying goodbye, an Iranian film crew bounced into his front yard to shoot a seven-part series on the thinking behind his new book on the history of Islam, and the critical moments of paradigm shifts. Over the following eighteen years, Hans Kung and I kept in contact and exchanged Christmas cards. Needless to say, I admired him greatly, and enjoyed his friendship, and was grateful for his critique.

What did this leg of the quest teach me, this quick trip to Istanbul, Geneva, and Tubingen? I learned that my idea was so large and complicated that major religious leaders find it hard to engage. I learned that there were professionals in the world of interfaith work who were light years ahead of me and who were willing to scratch out a few areas wherein I had better quickly move from ignorance to knowing. And I learned that I could not straddle the fence between a United Religions and a United Religions Initiative much longer. The time for committing to one or the other was fast approaching. And so was my trip to Rome and the Vatican.

Chapter 13
The Great Journey — Wrestling With Giants

Whoever was beaten by this Angel
(who often simply declined the fight)
went away proud and strengthened
and great from that harsh hand,
that kneaded him as if to change his shape.
Winning does not tempt that man.
This is how he grows: by being defeated, decisively,
by constantly greater beings.

Rainer Maria Rilke
The Man Watching

The line from Rilke's poem about Jacob wrestling with the angel, "This is how he grows, by being defeated decisively by ever greater giants," echoed in my mind as we flew off for the final legs of the quest, for appointments in the Vatican and Lambeth Palace. The big test!

I received an email from my friend, Archbishop William Levada of San Francisco, saying he had arranged an appointment for me at the Vatican. Mary and I found ourselves walking into the office of the Pontifical Council for Interreligious Dialogue, the office of Cardinal Francis Arinze and his Assistant, Archbishop Michael Fitzgerald. Going in, I figured that if the Roman Catholic Church refused to be a member of the World Council of Churches, an organization that did exist, who was I to hope that it would be part of a United Religions, which didn't exist? But why not plant a seed in the ground? And why not gain an understanding of their point of view regarding interfaith work? I had nothing to lose. Well, almost nothing!

I experienced a Saturday version of Cardinal Arinze and a Monday Cardinal Arinze. The Saturday one had no idea who I was or why I was there. He was most pleasant and had a great sense of humor. When I did get down to matters, he said that this deserved far more than the twenty minutes allotted and that I should come back on Monday for a thorough conversation with Archbishop Michael Fitzgerald, the Cardinal's assistant. Before leaving, he explained the Roman Catholic Church's operational framework for interreligious dialogue. The Vatican itself was involved in serious ecumenical dialogues with several Christian bodies and was involved with interfaith dialogues with several religions. If there was any demand or opportunity for international interfaith agendas, the Roman Catholic Church chose the World Conference of Religion and Peace to be its conduit. WCRP had a special sensitivity for the Vatican and had won its confidence. There was no need for the Vatican to be involved with any other group. At the end of our time, I left a copy of my Oxford talk.

On Monday while I was speaking with Archbishop Fitzgerald, Cardinal Arinze stormed into the room. He had read my Oxford talk, threw it on the table and announced that the Roman Catholic Church would never have anything to do with the United Religions. He stayed long enough for us to have an exchange about his reaction. Why? First of all, he said that Jesus Christ sent them out to evangelize the world, not to unite the religions. Then he went on to say that it would not be fair for a recent and small religion or a weird offshoot religion to be at a table as an equal partner with an historic, worldwide religion. Further he accentuated how profoundly committed the Roman Catholic Church is to its highly disciplined dialogues that already exist. Since Cardinal Arinze's name was often mentioned as a possible successor to Pope John Paul, II, I figured that I would have to "go back to the drawing board." Over the long haul, Cardinal Arinze's prediction did not completely hold up. Two Popes later, Pope Francis I turned out to be a friend of URI. In 2007, then a Cardinal in Buenos Aires, he invited me and several of my URI friends to have an interfaith prayer service with him in his cathedral in Buenos Aires. In addition, many Roman Catholic priests, nuns, Jesuits, Dominicans, bishops, and archbishops have served on URI's Global Council or Global Staff or have become members of URI Cooperation Circles.

As he was leaving, Cardinal Arinze said that his approach to the United Religions going forward would be the approach that Gamaliel took in Acts 5:38, 39 when he said, "Keep away from these men and let them alone; because if this plan is of human origin, it will fail; but if it is of God, you will not be able to overthrow them and you might find yourself fighting against God." Fair enough! And then while walking out of the room, he asked if we wanted to go to the Papal Audience in St. Peter's Square, two days thence with His Holiness John Paul II. "Why, yes, that would be a treat," we replied.

Obviously I was deeply shaken by this exchange. It raised a host of primitive questions. Was the United Religions that I was promoting "of God"? I do think that God burdened me with the message that religions have a vocation to serve together in addressing the hard issues of this world—including sectarian violence, environmental degradation, and human rights. Despite all of the unanswered questions for a future United Religions, and despite all of the heinous misuse of religion that could rush in under such a banner, I was still convinced that if religions could find a way to work with each other, the world would be enriched.

Then came the surprise of Wednesday, April 24. I walked over the Erba River Bridge to the Interfaith Office to pick up the tickets to the Papal Audience two days later. Interestingly, we weren't handed tickets but an invitation, whatever that meant. Friends in Rome warned us that people arrive early and that we would probably be in the distant orange section or the even more distant blue section, so please get there early and stand close to the route of the Popemobile. Figuring it to be in the mob scene of 25,000 people, I debated about wearing a sweater or a clerical collar and jacket, and finally settled on the latter.

At 10:00 a.m. we arrived at St. Peter's Square and showed our invitation to a policeman. He studied it for a while and sent us to another policeman. He studied our invitation and then passed us on to a member of the Swiss Guard. Finally, he passed us on to a man in a formal cutaway. He studied it and then started walking us up the center aisle and right up to the Papal Throne where we were seated immediately to the right of it. Next to the Pope were a few Cardinals and Archbishops, and then behind them were Her Excellency, Mary Taylor Swing, and the Bishop of California. Of course Mary chose the seat on the end facing the throne, but a dutiful usher reversed our seating. When the sun began to beat down, the Cardinals and Archbishops were moved to a shady area, and there were the two of us next to the Pope. Oh, my! What an honor! I was accustomed to traversing the world at 30,000 feet, but I had never been at this kind of altitude.

Afterwards we had our pictures taken with the Pope, kissed his hand, and brought greetings to him from San Francisco. I looked at Mary and thought that she was adjusting well to her ecclesiastical prominence, perhaps too well. Perhaps I will have to buy her an amethyst ring with a seal on it for Christmas. Some years later, just before His Holiness John Paul II died, I had a private audience with him. He whispered in my ear, "All the best, Yank."

We had one more adventure before leaving town. I miscalculated the time of our airplane departure, so when I finally looked at the ticket, I discovered that the plane was leaving immanently. We went into panic packing mode, and the little round jewel box in which Mary kept the jewels she had collected during this trip, rolled off the bed and hid under the bed. We didn't realize this until Mary started looking for her jewelry in the cab that was racing toward the airport. The driver phoned our Sant' Anna Hotel, and the concierge promised to mail the box of jewels to our home in San Francisco. It never arrived. After many months we gave up hoping. Later on, almost one year to the day, I walked into the Sant' Anna Hotel to make a reservation for a future stay. The man behind the counter said, "Bishop Swing! We have your wife's jewels. We were afraid to send them to you, for fear that someone at the airport might just steal them. So we have been waiting for your return." Some you lose; some you find.

On the next day, at our hotel in London, an email from Mother Teresa was waiting. She was not going to send anyone to our Charter Writing Session next summer. News must travel fast along the Vatican grapevine. Anyway, I now had the distinction of being the only person in the world rejected by Mother Teresa.

On Friday, April 26, 1996, Mary and I were warmly greeted at Lambeth Palace by Archbishop George Carey who could not have been more engaging and supportive. He noted that in his first five years as Archbishop of Canterbury, he had to give more and more time to interfaith matters. He imagined that a strong point for a United Religions would be the proliferation of interfaith demands and initiatives. There needed to be one place that would serve as a clearinghouse for all of the religious leaders.

He did have one caution. When I mentioned the possibility of people from different religions praying together, he got very nervous. He thought that this was a delicate area and warned that proceeding with this idea might cause people to think of the United Religions as blending the integrity of each group. He wanted us to avoid the label of syncretism.

The obvious questions caught his interest: questions of representation, fundamentalists, other interfaith efforts, San Francisco, and whether or not to field-test the idea. He was sad about the Vatican's reaction and advised me to work only with the American Roman Catholics at the beginning—and perhaps in the long run, the Vatican might come around. But the fact that Hans Kung had expressed so much concern for this idea impressed him.

And finally he asked me if I was going home encouraged at the end of a long journey?

This simple question was just too big for me at that moment. I had seen so much, been so inspired, been so deflated, traveled so hard, wrestled with the vision so strenuously, that I was a little in the fog of dislocation. I knew that I would carry on in the future and proceed where the vision led me. But it was not a matter of being encouraged or discouraged. It was a matter of coming to grips with the complicated realities that surround an authentic vision. I couldn't afford to be encouraged or discouraged. I had to reach down inside myself to see what I had left in terms of energy and resolve. Intuitively, what I sensed was that whatever I was pursuing, I could no longer pursue it singularly. From now on, I needed to be part of a team that would make it happen, so I needed to invest more in creating the team than promoting the vision. Three months earlier I had flown away on a quest with high hopes for the participation of religious leaders. Soon my airplane would arrive back in San Francisco and I would have high hopes for the grassroots peoples of faith. Travel has a way of changing one's mind.

Before setting off, I had received a letter from a friend named Paul Andrews. Paul said that my upcoming journey made him think of the story of the adventurer Magellan who was convinced that existing circumferences and boundaries of the world were all wrong. Magellan didn't think that the world was flat, and so he sailed out without a map. Paul said that all Magellan had, "was a faith that the world was round and the determination to keep going ahead at all costs.... It was his faith in the oneness of the world, and the ultimate success of his expedition, that made him the world's first true global citizen." As I took off, I was flattered that Paul held me up to such a comparison. At the end of my journey, I wondered what Paul might be thinking now. The world of religions dealing with each other was still flat, but some thoughts of oneness and collaboration were stirred. And, as the old baseball saying puts it, "The game ain't over yet."

When our airplane's wheels touched the tarmac of the San Francisco Airport on Tuesday, April 30, 1996, I was dreaming about sleeping in my own bed and getting back to my regular routine. And it was just then that Mary grabbed my hand and said, "Let's stay on the plane and go around the world again." That lady has a lot of Magellan in her.

Chapter 14
The First Global Summit and the
First of the Defining Partnerships

In 1945, when the United Nations was finalizing and signing
its Charter, the Fairmont Hotel figured prominently as a gathering location in San Francisco. What better place to have the
First Global Summit of the initiative for a United Religion?
Dr. Robert Muller, former Under-Secretary of the United Nations, brought along with him a special chair in June 1996. It
was a replica of the one used by President George Washington at the first meeting of the United States Congress in 1789.
Benjamin Franklin used to stare at the bronze depiction of a
half-sun at the chair's top wondering if the sun was rising or
setting. At the end of the Congress and the beginning of the
United States, Franklin was thoroughly convinced that the
half-sun on the chair was rising. How's that for an appropriate prop? At the end of our time together, all fifty-six of us
sat in the chair, one at a time, and received a blessing from
everyone else, a blessing of new birth.

Charlotte Mailliard Swig, who often served as Chief of Protocol for the City of San Francisco and for the State of California, invited us all to her penthouse for a celebration. High
above the San Francisco Bay, we were thrilled to have such a
commanding perspective, to see so many bridges and so
much beauty.

The people who attended were neither great religious leaders nor deputies from leading faith traditions. But they
were leaders in their own fields and were drawn to the possibility of a United Religions. Some of those who traveled
from afar to be there were Dr. Jane Pratt, CEO of the Mountain Institute; the Venerable Chung Ok Lee of Korea; Juliet

Hollister of the Temple of Understanding; Bawa Jain, a Jain interfaith leader; Sister Jayanti Kirpalani of the Brahma Kumaris; John Caron, a Connecticut businessman; Jim Lord, an international philanthropist; Bettina Gray, a video journalist; sister Joan Chatfield, a Maryknoll sister; Joseph Boehle, a Ph.D. student from Germany; Deborah Moldow of the World Peace Prayer Society; Father Louis Dolan of the Temple of Understanding; David Storey, an English interfaith leader; Father Gerald O'Rourke of Ireland; and many others.

At this First Global Summit, I welcomed the fifty-six persons gathered to start the Charter Writing process with these words:

"I am convinced that someday there will be a United Religions. There has to be. There is not going to be a time in the near future when one religion converts, conquers, subjugates all of the other religions. Furthermore, religions are going to have to learn to live together. No longer can one religion use terror, law, threat to excise other religions from its territory. Communication crosses borders and enters homes, so people are now exposed to other religions. The sooner we find a way for religions to share the same geographic space, the sooner life will be enhanced. The sooner we can get religions to come together to serve the common good, the sooner global issues will have a chance for solution. I know that eventually there will be a United Religions because there has to be. The question is, sooner or later?

"At the beginning of the twentieth century there was a time when human beings knew in their bones that we should fly. So all kinds of people glued feathers to their arms, climbed to the top of the barn, began flapping, and jumped off. And sure enough, right around then, we learned to fly. I don't mind standing in front of you today, smelling of feathers and sticking with glue. I'll tell you right now, I'm jumping. This Summit comes down to one invitation to you for the creation of a United Religions. "Come, let's fly!"

Three days of meetings at the Fairmont Hotel resulted in no Charter, but several innovations were forthcoming. First of all, we became something of a community. Just as the San Francisco interfaith leaders in 1993 bonded together to pull off the U.N. 50th, and just as six people met in my living room in 1995 after the big event and decided to "go for it," all but one of these people at the Fairmont jumped into the quest. For a while, they became the "we" of URI. They brought lots of experience in working with NGOs and non-for-profits, and they brought great energy. In the end, there was a limit to their backing. They were willing to help in most all ways except in raising money for the enterprise. So their initial support came in the form of wisdom and council.

Second, they helped us think through what the URI was to become. After hearing the results of my world travels, they did not know exactly what form the URI would take, but they were clear about who should be invited to belong: A) Grassroots members of all of the religions of the world, with no distinction between ancient and modern, small and large, popular or scorned—all. B) Women and men, equally. When I traveled the world to talk with religious leaders, I spoke with men. There would never be peace among religions if only men sat at the table. C) Not only should people of all religions be invited, but also people of all indigenous traditions. In some cases, tribal spirituality is far older than some religions. And the invitation extended even further, to people who say, "I am spiritual but not religious," such as humanists. If we were going to open the door, we were going to open it all the way.

It was clear that up-front money was essential for getting started. So we all agreed that I should take out a million dollar line of credit to personally underwrite all of the activities that would be needed if URI ever were to become a reality. Further, we recommended that, in order to get started, four people should be hired as staff for a URI, an office should be rented, and the staff should carry out interfaith conferences throughout the world, as well as get URI established as an official, recognized nonprofit organization in the U.S., complete with a 501 (c) (3) status.

We were not successful in writing a Charter at this gathering, so we decided to plan a charter-writing session in the Bay Area in June 1997, with an expanded group. Our aim was to have the Charter written in 1997, and the organization up and running by the millennium year 2000, preferably by June 26, the anniversary of the founding of the U.N.

When the conference ended, fifty-five of fifty-six people endorsed that course of action by consensus, and that group never met again. Because it did not represent an ongoing seat of authority, the group scattered as a body, and its individuals were left asking how each one might help to get URI launched. In the meantime, I was still holding 100 percent of the responsibility and authority for the idea of a United Religions, and for the creation of a United Religions Initiative.

The "we" of URI were now four people in an office answerable to themselves (one to another) and to me, doing everything they could think of to get organized, to become visible, and to attract a world of participants. I couldn't help them much because I was back running the Diocese of California. But they and I checked in with each other often.

The boss in the office was the Episcopal Rev. Charles P. Gibbs, who had to negotiate his leave-taking from his parish of the Incarnation in order to take this job. This was tricky for him because he had just gotten back from a sabbatical. It was tricky business for me as the Bishop of that congregation. All rectors in the Diocese of California have to pledge to their parishes that they will return to their parish for one year following a sabbatical. In this case, I had to go to the parish and ask if they would release Charles from this obligation so he could become URI's first Executive Director. In truth, the parish was very supportive of this exceptional action. It also created years of poking fun at one another—"the Bishop stole our wonderful rector." Seventeen years later, upon Charles's retirement from URI, I contacted the parish, and said they could have him back.

Charles was one of the first people to volunteer for the U.N. 50th interfaith ceremony and to further the vision of the United Religions. When I traveled the world, it was Charles with whom I communicated and who kept the business aspect going. So he was my obvious choice. Once he took over as Executive Director, it ceased to be "my URI." The natural leap was for Charles to be the face and voice of the enterprise at conferences, and I was still the face and voice of URI at international meetings, in fund-raising, and in speaking to the public at large. In the narrowest sense, it was "our URI," Charles and mine.

Money! I had seen enough of the world to understand that international interfaith work is money. At the time, established international interfaith communities had access to a great deal of money. The largest international interfaith organization at that time had the financial backing of the Vatican, a large new Buddhist religion in Japan, and the king of Saudi Arabia. At the same time, the Rev. Sun Myung Moon invested millions and millions of his money to branch into interfaith work. As for me and my United Religions idea, I had a line of credit for a million dollars that Mary and I were obliged to pay back. The bottom line in interfaith work is, if you have money, you do it. If you don't have money, you talk. And the world is made up of lots of talkers. The URI was not going to happen unless someone stepped forward with sufficient money or sufficient commitment to raise the money. No one was there but me, and if I truly believed in this, I had to gamble our home and all of our assets as well as the prospect that we would be paying off this debt for the rest of our lives. Otherwise URI would never get off of the ground.

We needed to get real and we did. Charles took off in the world carrying on URI events in various countries while I took off in the world when I could, trying to spread the possibility of a United Religions or a United Religions Initiative. Meanwhile, "the meter was running."

Thankfully, there was a surprise factor. While I was on the trip around the world, a reporter in San Francisco wrote an article about my journey for a wire service. The only newspaper in the country that picked up the article was the Cleveland Plain Dealer. They ran it as a filler item on the business and finance page, of all places. Dr. David Cooperrider of Case Western School of Management's Social Innovations in Global Management (SIGMA) program saw the item. He thought it was the most important social innovation he had ever heard of, and he wanted to help. He wrote a letter offering his complete assistance and his innovative organizational design method, called Appreciative Inquiry. He volunteered to bring along Ph.D. students and to introduce this method into all of our conferences in the future. Bottom line: he energized and revolutionized our work. When Charles and the staff ventured off into the world to begin United Religions interfaith conferences, they leaned heavily on David Cooperrider's Appreciative Inquiry. Later on, when the Charter was being written, we all leaned on David for wisdom. And whenever we had to put on a large event in the world, we leaned on David's staff to make it happen. David came from out of the blue, from an amazing set of coincidences. And we never would have succeeded without him. He opened our eyes, our hearts, and lots of doors.

Of the many revolutionary ideas that David brought to the table was his firm belief that we don't get far by trying to fix the problems of the past, but instead we need to focus on the highest aspirations for the future, and allow these to lead us into fresh possibilities. His accent is always on appreciation of the richness that all people bring to new creations. And his genius is how to mine the mother lode of principled input of personal values that can be emancipated and put into motion.

David was a FedEx miracle. Fortunately his contribution to URI has already been chronicled in a splendid book entitled *Birth of a Global Community: Appreciative Inquiry in Action,* written by Charles Gibbs and Sally Mahé. I shudder to think of where we would have been without David. We opened up an office and scheduled interfaith events all over the world, but without Appreciative Inquiry we would have had little to offer our participants. It is natural to see from the viewpoint of the authors—who had the responsibility of carrying out these conferences—that the URI is an outgrowth of Appreciative Inquiry. Although there were other profound partnerships that fashioned URI, foundationally, David Cooperrider and Appreciative Inquiry (AI) were the first and most influential, providing a young URI with its DNA.

I felt at home with AI from the beginning because it resonated with my experience in parishes and organizations, and with some of my training. While a young priest, I participated in and led design skills conferences, sensitivity training, seminars focused on how people function in small groups, and in organizational development. So when David came along talking about Discovery, Dreaming, Designing, and Destiny (4-D), I could jump right in. This was not alien territory.

What AI did was to reverse the order of URI's reality. In theory, I had anticipated that a Charter would come first, and then the Charter would give birth to a community. What actually happened was that when we gathered to begin writing the Charter, a community broke out.

Beyond organizational design, an organization cultivates a prevailing spirit. The spirit that emerged in URI was inspired greatly by the kindness and profound respect that David and Charles seeded throughout the world, beginning in such far-flung places as Venezuela, Oxford, and New York. It culminated in the three-year Charter-writing effort, and prevailed at the meetings of subsequent Global

Assemblies. The Charter of URI was cradled in the spirit of the URI. And the spirit of URI was fashioned chiefly in the kindness and care of Charles Gibbs and David Cooperrider in URI's leadership, and also by Sally Mahé, Paul Andrews, and Barbara Hartford in the office. To this day, if you go into a meeting of any of the hundreds of the basic units of URI (which are now called Cooperation Circles), in any of the almost one hundred countries that URI operates in, something of their collective spirit will be present.

In those early years, the leadership conversation was among Charles, David and myself. And we were all traveling the world at a pretty fast pace.

Chapter 15
Around the World Again for the First Time

No sooner was the June 1996 Summit over than I accepted a last-minute invitation to attend the Global Conference of the International Association for Religious Freedom (IARF) at Wonkwang University, Daejeon, Korea. Why? Because I had a backlog of places I needed to visit in the Far East on behalf of URI, and such a trip would afford me conversations with a host of religious leaders who had a history with interfaith matters. Thus, I was making this journey as a pilgrim, to learn and to show respect.

In addition, I was making this journey as someone who had just started an interfaith movement and had backed it with my name and all of my financial resources and risks. Thus I was the ambassador of the United Religions Initiative, and I wanted to get our story out into the interfaith community. I had been offered an opportunity to speak at the IARF gathering and couldn't miss that opportunity to announce that URI was officially in business.

Ambiguity would dog my every step on this trip and for the rest of my life. Yes, I realized that what we had started was a grassroots movement (URI). But I could not let go of the dream of a United Religions (UR). I tried as hard as I could to straddle these contradictory foci. I wanted to provoke thought about something larger than had ever existed, and at the same time, I needed to announce the arrival of a global grassroots organization. I felt that God had put a dream in my heart and I simply could not abandon it, even if it made me seem foolish and naïve to interfaith veterans.

In Tokyo I met with officers of the Rissho Kosei-Kai, sometimes referred to as Buddhist, sometimes as a New Religion, which had an interfaith department and a recent strong interfaith record of involvement and funding. What quickly became clear was that they were deeply tied in with another international interfaith organization, the World Conference of Religion and Peace (WCRP) and weren't interested in expanding their commitments. That was certainly understandable.

Also in Tokyo, I met with the Anglican Archbishop of Japan. I looked at him and said, "Jim, is that you?" He looked at me and asked, "Bill, is that you?" To our amazement it turned out that he had run a pool hall at Kenyon College in Gambier, Ohio in 1954 when I was a student there. I often went to his pool hall and we were buddies then. Now, he promised that although he is an interfaith leader in Japan affiliated with another group (WCRP), he would put in good words for URI.

Outside of Kyoto, in the Oomoto estate in Kameoka, I met the marvelous Shinto people of Oomoto. In 1925 their leader had advanced an idea of something like a United Religions, so they were keen to hear what I had to say. Since then, they have sponsored numerous interfaith gatherings. This was the first of numerous visits back and forth between Oomoto and URI. Nevertheless, their culture is centered not in grassroots people, but in a conference of elders. Try as I might for many years, nothing ever materialized, although they and we have sympathetic hearts for each other.

Planting seeds in good soil, and being patient, brings results. Seventeen years later the URI was graced by two centers of work in Japan.

The interfaith backdrop for this whole trip was the power and reach of the World Conference of Religion and Peace (WCRP). They had cornered the interfaith market in this part of the world with their good work and diligence in building up a regional office. Even the head of the IARF, which has extremely close ties with WCRP, warned me in Korea that unless URI comes up with "a clear new vision, new money, and a new constituency" we would merely be taken as an upstart rival to WCRP. Those words have had a truthful ring. For many years, URI was seen as an upstart rival to WCRP around the world, and yes, we did come up with a new vision, new money, and a new constituency. In the end, the ugly parts of rivalry were lessened because WCRP aimed mainly for religious leaders while URI aimed mainly for grassroots people. But back in August 1996, I would be about as welcome as "a skunk at a garden party."

The big moment that I had been waiting for in Korea was an interview with the Prime Master Chwasan of the Won Buddhists. Naturally, he was a great friend of WCRP, but the thing that intrigued him about me was the idea of a United Religions. He had several points that he wanted to make: 1) He had given several speeches over the past years calling for the creation of a United Religions. Speaking about it is the proper way to proceed. 2) Patience is most important in arriving at a UR. 3) There should be no competition, stress, fighting, anxious striving in bringing about a UR (he had heard that my presence had aroused competition). 4) It is critical to lay a solid foundation, and 5) It is critical that the wide variety of religions need to be brought on board, and most importantly, the leadership for making decisions needs to be in the hands of the many and not just one.

I thanked him for his wisdom and comments, and risking impertinence (he was seated high on a throne while I was seated on the floor) I wanted to make a few points of my own. 1) A United Religions cannot be the genius of one religious tradition or controlled by one religious tradition. 2) Whereas his gift was one of patience, my gift was one of impatience. I was impatient because of all of the unbridled harm that religions do without any seat of accountability. 3) A United Religions would come long after I am gone. But I am willing to lay down my life as bridge to that eventual day. 4) I don't see myself as the great originator of the United Religions idea, but only as a servant of it. 5) A process for getting there will not come out of thin air, but must be created, and only the religions themselves can rightfully take the role of decision-making by virtue of writing a Charter, signing it, and carrying it out.

One person witnessing this conversation was ecstatic. Another thought it had been a good session. I was devastated. It seemed to me that someone had gotten Master Chwasan's ear to warn him that I was trouble, and threatening his exclusive rights to the idea. He mentioned that a United Religions was the highest dharma, conversation between heaven and earth. I only wish that I could have had the opportunity of extended conversations with him to dig deeper into the heart of the matter. As it was, I benefitted from hearing his perspective.

Chapter 16
The Year That Wouldn't End

In 1996 another accidental invitation came in—this time to Rome. A well-positioned lay order, the Sant'Egidio Community, for the first time invited the Presiding Bishop of the Episcopal Church to attend its annual interfaith gathering in Rome in October. The Presiding Bishop couldn't make it, so he asked the bishop of Chicago to represent him. A seminary professor persuaded the Presiding Bishop that since I was involved deeply in interfaith work, I, too, should attend. And so it was. Although it did not fit into my work schedule, I cut short my attendance at the meeting of the House of Bishops of the Episcopal Church of the U.S. and headed to Rome.

What was that like? It was like dining at the celebrated restaurant Villa dei Quintilii on the Via Appia Antica, like attending meetings in Palazzo della Cancelleria, like being invited to an evening reception at Castel Sant'Angelo, erected in 130 A.D. by the Roman Emperor Hadrian, where popes have been sheltered from attacks and can take secret passages that still go to the Vatican. And most glorious of all, it was like coming out of a church service with leaders of all of the religions on earth and marching down streets of Rome filled with thousands of cheering people, and ending up in the Piazza Santa Maria, with all of the leaders lighting candles of peace. This was interfaith as I had never imagined. It was a picture to carry for a lifetime.

Of course the entire conference was not all glory. There were lots of talks and posturing, and everyone was put in their place historically and for other purposes. Nevertheless, the wonderful people of Sant'Egidio provided a welcome and a hospitality that were breathtaking.

Here is a sample of one of the conversations: Mary was speaking with a Sikh leader from New Delhi who said, "You know your husband is crazy and you are crazy. The United Religions idea is so big that it is crazy. You have to be crazy to keep on working on it. But all great ideas are pushed by people who are crazy. Your craziness is needed."

Although that generous critique was gentle compared to others I received, it was clear that I was winning a little bit of respect because I refused to go away.

Interestingly, throughout the conference many speakers came close, so close to coming to the same conclusion as I. For instance, one editor said, "We have to set up new forms of worldwide governance to address worldwide religious problems." Another said, "Forces of war today are powerful. Religious force for peace needs to be mobilized and needs to be at least equally powerful." Someone else said, "Every country is being attacked by invading armies of refugees and/or invading values transmitted by way of video, music and movies. Religions need to address this collectively." Having said that, no one had a speck of imagination for thinking beyond what exists today in terms of faith and interfaith.

Here's what I wrote going home: "Will the United Religions Initiative 2000 lead eventually to the creation of a United Religions? Before this trip, I figured the odds to be about three trillion to one. But now I figure the odds are three trillion to two. Why? Because God wants it to happen. I'm going to let the string run out figuring that this has the hint of Divine intent. On this trip I found young people who are spontaneously moving in this direction with deep commitment. Not yet all the way to a UR, but on the way, and bringing the right instincts for hospitality, negotiation, and reconciliation. Even wise old people are coming very close to giving voice to such a vision. Meanwhile, we are collecting a small cadre who "get it" and another audience that is at least impressed by our precociousness. So, by Christmas I think, the odds will be three trillion to five."

With the end of 1996 approaching, I figured that my travels were finally over. But, no. There was a quick trip to Washington, D.C. with Charles Gibbs. We met with URI sympathizers, with a con man who promised us lots of money just before he went to jail, with a Lutheran bishop, with a leader in Religion and Ecology, with the remarkable head of the Mountain Institute, with the folks of the Millennium Institute, with professors from Georgetown and George Washington Universities, with the head of the Center for Strategic and International Studies, and with the Board of Washington's Interfaith Conference. It was a breathless journey, as they all were, and one that vastly broadened my horizons while I was planting seeds.

Meanwhile, back home in San Francisco, Mayor Willie Brown was taking a small group to Paris for a Sister City Tour. His Chief of Protocol promised that if I went, I would have an opportunity to meet with the Roman Catholic, Muslim, and Protestant leaders of France. I said yes, and off we went on oil heir Getty's private jet. Keeping to the Rome theme of opulence, we ended up at the Ballet de L'Opéra National de Paris, Hôtel de Ville (City Hall as you have never seen a city hall), the United States' Ambassadors' Residence, the Cercle de L'Union Interalliée, and the American Cathedral in Paris. I had to smile thinking that I started this year on the banks of the

Pamba River in India and ended it on the left bank of the Seine. Although not all of the religious leaders I had hoped to meet were available, I was able to make contact with a goodly number. So it was worth the time to squeeze in one more trip in an amazing year for me and for URI/UR.

1996—the year of URI's birth. This was the year of the founding summit, the personal financial loan, the first staff headed by an Executive Office, and the first URI interfaith conferences around the world. But URI did not come from nothing. URI came from the vision of a United Religions. That vision was the overarching source of heightened imagination and audacious reach. I traveled almost 100,000 miles that year proclaiming the possibility of a United Religions and readying the world for what would be coming next in the URI. At year's end I was exhausted, elated, chastened, tested, knowledgeable, and supremely optimistic. I couldn't wait for the next installment. URI was no longer all about me. Now it was about the "we" who would be emerging.

Chapter 17
The Second Global Summit and The Stanford Miracle

There were three Global Summits held at Stanford University in the summers of 1997, 1998, and 1999, and like most everything else on the journey of founding URI, I aimed at one thing and ended up hitting another. Or in this case, I aimed for these gatherings to be Charter Writing Sessions, but they were nothing of the kind. Oh, we held up streams of paper to write on and prepared agendas for Charter Writing, but in truth, when the entire group was together, we just could not get to the first step of Charter Writing. Instead we became a global community where people began to trust each other, and developed a unifying passion to create a United Religions Initiative around the world.

As Charles and the staff circled the world conducting URI conferences, they ran into a wealth of human resource that was ripe and ready for a URI. These people in turn were invited to attend URI summits on the campus of Stanford University. These events were not like five Bay Area people in my living room in June of 1995. Not like fifty-six people at the Fairmont Hotel in 1996. By the summers of 1997, 1998, and 1999, hundreds of people from all over the world wanted to give birth to a URI, and showed up. And they became the URI global community. It was a marvel to behold, and absolutely thrilling for the participants. We could no longer be faulted for being just an idea without any legs. URI was no longer something in my mind; I could now look out and see it in the assemblage. URI now had its own mind and its own constituency.

Many factors went into this miraculous success, namely Charles and the staff, David Cooperrider and the SIGMA people, Appreciative Inquiry, my financial line of credit from the bank, a large group of volunteers that had formed, and the rich quality of people who attended. These were breathtaking occasions. So many conversations among people who had never talked with anyone from some of the other religions! So much imagination in dreaming of what could be! And so much spontaneous fun and creativity on the nights of celebrating!

We learned a lot about hospitality. Instead of focusing on who should be at the interfaith table, we began to focus on what meal should be served at that table. We did not want to spend primary time fine-tuning pronouncements; instead, we first wanted to show extravagant hospitality to those who make pronouncements. Our aim was to start out with an ever-expanding community of interfaith hospitality. This was to be an outgrowth of Appreciative Inquiry. Hospitality should prove our existence: I welcome, therefore I am.

As for praying together or sharing devotional practices, that was tricky. If we had developed some kind of spiritual practice, we would quickly be accused of starting a new religion, something we most definitely did not want to do. But when people who practice different faiths get together and share the depths of their hearts, it is impossible to mute all sacred music and wisdom. David Cooperrider came up with a helpful thought, saying, "Each of our communities of faith have special gifts in our traditions, beliefs, and values, and the best of these need to be brought to the arena of interfaith cooperation and action. As you think about your community of faith, what are some of the most positive qualities or gifts that could assist a global community in creating a United Religions Initiative?"

We intended to be a global network of cooperative action but, almost despite ourselves, we also became a community of people sensitive to the matters of the spirit. One of my lasting memories is of Marcus Braybrooke sitting on the steps of a Stanford building saying, "This isn't an interfaith organization; this is a spiritual movement." There was some truth to that statement. We did learn to take off our shoes when approaching the holy ground of others; that was the only way that we could hold together a world full of people with fervent and differing beliefs, and at the same time avoid creating a religion.

As for prevalent leadership styles, I was right at home. Everyone got into the act of shared leadership. When I was a parish priest in Washington, D.C., my personal leadership motto was: anything that is worth doing, is worth doing poorly. Because if you do it poorly in front of a large group of competent people, someone invariably will step forward and volunteer to do it right. When I gave away authority and trusted other people to do their jobs, I was amazed at the high quality of what they produced. Of course, a certain amount of screening and training was needed, and the people had to be held accountable. But I had seen great things come from shared leadership and a supportive community. So I was quite at home with the kind of leadership style that David and Charles were promoting.

My leadership style blended right in, although it was unrehearsed and unscripted. At the final session of the conference, a question was directed to me by one of the participants. "What do we do now?" We were at the end of our dreaming and had nothing to show for our big talk. Zero impact on the world after three years of gathering and hundreds of thousands of dollars in debt. The Charter had not been completed, and everything or nothing were staring us in the face. Here I said words that came to me in a flash. "I, William Swing, deputize you to go home and start the United Religions right where you live." It was akin to the flight attendant declaring, "You are free to get up and move about the cabin." All of the seat belts of religious restraint were unloosed, and everyone was left to figure out exactly what he or she needed to do with this freedom to be creative in the field of religion that had seemed so ossified. No directives from headquarters. From now on, someone is a leader only if someone leads. That was the "Big Bang" moment when raw energy was unleashed. A little sentence, unprepared and in context of a perfect storm of converging favorable factors, elicited the pent-up genius of people who had hearts for interfaith potential.

I need to add that it wasn't all about URI. In our midst at Stanford was a brilliant young man, Eboo Patel from Chicago, who felt like we were going to take a long time getting the URI up and running. But he had a passion to do interfaith youth work in the U.S. immediately. So he wanted to start the Interfaith Youth Corps. He did, and it became significant for thousands of people in this country. He even became an advisor to a president of the United States, Barack Obama, on interfaith matters. But at that time he only had a dream and no money. I got a loan for $25,000 and gave it to him to get started. Today I take great comfort in knowing that not only did URI succeed, but we helped Eboo's dream succeed as well.

I would be remiss if I didn't say that we also had to face up to our limitations, what we could do together as well as what we couldn't. In one of our Stanford summits, a young man from San Francisco asked for permission to speak. He started into a long, impassioned cry for support for himself, a gay man, and for all of the homosexuals who have experienced bitter discrimination at the hands of religions. His tears and plea ended with people from all over the world streaming out of the doors and making plans to bow out of URI immediately. This was an especially hard scene for me in the late 1990s. I had been moving delicately and firmly in the Episcopal Diocese of California on the issue of gay ordination. At Stanford, the Muslim, Sikhs, Hindus, and others were outraged by the young man's remarks. What to do now? I couldn't let one divisive moment destroy all of the work that had gone into getting everyone together. So I begged everyone to come back together so that we could talk our way through this critical moment. We did exactly that. The result was similar to the result over all of the contentious religious issues that vehemently separated us. We figured that we could not afford to solve all of the past religious and current moral and social problems before we became an authentic community. We had to lay aside, for the moment, the righteous arguments that divide us, in order to begin to form an appreciative community. That community, in time, had the promise of changing the culture of religious interaction and of providing a more creative setting for people to learn to live together. So on that day, the URI decided not to be primarily an advocacy group, but rather to invest itself in reconciliation.

Chapter 18
The Second Defining Partnership and Growing a Presence

Early on we stumbled into a partnership that separated URI from all other similar interfaith groups. Because we failed miserably at coming up with an appropriate Charter, we desperately looked around for help. A little team was commissioned with the task of finding assistance in writing a Charter. That search lead to an interview with the man who was a key creator of the internationally-accepted Visa Card. His name is Dee Hock.

Dee has been guided by a method of problem solving that honors both chaos and order. He blends chaos and order together into something he calls Chaordic Alliance, an innovative method of organizational design with which we were about to become fully familiar. He immediately had my attention because, as a parish priest, I always thought that one of my duties was to allow a certain degree of creative chaos in a community. Then, as we struggled with how to incorporate the best of the chaos into the life of the parish, we most often came out into a way toward a new and higher order. It seemed to me that we grew incrementally as we lurched from chaos to order—and then back to chaos—and then order. So when Dee started talking, I listened.

What really sold me on Dee was a story he told. At the very beginning of Visa, he went around the world and tried to talk bank officers into taking the Visa Card. Once, he was in Germany, talking with the President of Deutsche Bank. No sale. The president vehemently slapped his fist into his other hand and declared: "There will never be a Visa Card in the Germany!" To which Dee said, "When every country in the world has the Visa Card, there will be the first country and later, the last country. Why shouldn't the last country in the world be Germany? When every bank in the world has the Visa Card, there will be the first bank, and later the last bank. Why shouldn't Deutsche Bank be the last bank? And when every bank President in the world has the Visa Card in his own pocket, there will be the first president and later the last. And why shouldn't the last bank president in the world be you?"

The challenge that he faced in selling a concept to organizations all over the world matched mine in degree of difficulty, and our resolve to meet the challenge and prevail was recognizable in each other. I spent a large part of the next two years of my life with this man, sitting at a table. I loved his boldness. It helped me tolerate the tediousness of the work.

I wondered if what he had done in banking could also be done in the field of religion.

"Could it?" I asked.

"If you want to create something that is non-bureaucratic, decentralized, and where the greatest amount of authority is located in the smallest unit—yes," he said, "If you want something that is organized more in the organic way that nature organizes than in the hierarchical way that the Industrial Revolution taught us to organize—then yes." He added a condition. "But," he said, "in order to produce such a Charter in the world of religion, you and your friends will have to sit at a table with me for a couple of years and pore over the possibilities."

Impossible, I thought. I told Dee I was a working man, that as the Bishop of the Diocese of California I had a day job overseeing 40 schools, 87 churches, 400 priests and deacons, 35,000 parishioners, housing for 1,500 homeless people a night, and on and on. For Dee, that was no excuse. "You've got to sit at the table," he insisted. So from 1997 to 2000, I joined thirteen other people committed to spending a lot of time with Dee Hock and his Chaordic Alliance experts.

After founding the Visa Card, Dee went to his ranch in Pescadero, California in 1984 to try to enlarge on his thinking about institutional change. In a speech at the State of the World Forum in San Francisco, in 1997, he said, "...[I]t doesn't take much thought to realize we are in the midst of a global epidemic of institutional failure. Not just failure in the limited sense of collapse, such as the Soviet Union or corporate bankruptcy, but the more pervasive, pernicious form: institutions increasingly unable to achieve the purpose for which they were created, yet continuing to exist as they increasingly devour resources, demean people, and destroy the environment." In that speech he also said, "We do not have an education problem, or a health care problem, or a welfare problem, a political problem, an economic problem, a peace problem and/or a population problem. At bottom, we have an institutional problem, and until we deal with it, we will struggle in vain with all of the symptoms."

When I mentioned to Dee that religions deal with one another in a pernicious and self-denigrating way, he suggested that he could be of help. What we needed to do, according to him, was to create a chaordic institution with a fine balance of chaos and order. We had to free ourselves from the command and control concepts of organizational and hierarchical religious management models, and allow for self-organizing, distributive governance, seamless blend of cooperation and competition, and be infinitely malleable and extremely durable at the same time.

It would not be much of a stretch to say that the theology of URI was mostly fashioned by a banker, Dee Hock. He said to the State of the World Forum and later to us at URI, "In my view, we are at that precise point in time when a four-hundred-year-old (Industrial Revolution) age is rattling in its deathbed, and another age is struggling to be born. A shifting of consciousness, culture, society, and institutions enormously greater than the world has ever experienced! Ahead, the possibility of liberty, community, and ethics such as the world has never known, and a harmony with nature, with one another, and with the divine intelligence such as the world had ever dreamed."

So he took us by the hand, and led us through a purpose statement and then to the creation of twenty-one principles. Then, to the collection of the initial members who became a community. Then, to a perception of a structure that could be trusted as our concept, which morphed into an actual structure. And finally, to a practice that put all of the other components into play. It was with the tutelage of Dee Hock that we figured out that the greatest authority within URI was going to be invested in the smallest unit, namely the Cooperation Circle, which would be made up of at least seven people from at least three different traditions. Cooperation Circles would self-organize, self-fund, and self-govern. In all of this we were definitely not modeling ourselves on anything that existed, although Alcoholics Anonymous and the Rotary Club have organizational models that approach URI's. We built URI on the hopes that the world of religions was in for a new and unprecedented day.

Imagine trying to find a value or a principle with which every religion and indigenous tribe and ethical humanist in the world would agree. Imagine trying to find words to express the principle in such a clear way that everyone would understand and could buy into it, if they so choose. Imagine coming up with an organizational design that would give immediate access to anyone in the world who would want to affiliate. How's that for a challenge? It took us three years to write a one-sentence Purpose Statement—one single sentence. This is what we came up with:

"The purpose of the United Religions Initiative is to promote enduring, daily interfaith cooperation, to end religiously motivated violence, and to create cultures of peace, justice and healing for the earth and all living beings."

Even so, that was accomplished only at the very last minute, with gut-wrenching compromises, just before going to press with the charter that would go out worldwide so all URI participants would have a chance to read it prior to signing it.

Of course, there was a tug-of-war over whose charter this was. Was it the product of fourteen people sitting at a table for a couple of years? Or was it the product of voices from around the world, and specifically the now-burgeoning URI global community? In reality, it was both. There was tension between bringing everyone in, and at the same time having certain officials craft a final product. That tension became a universal characteristic of the organization, just part of being URI.

A Charter could be written in an afternoon. Just use bland words like, "toleration," "understanding," and "cooperation," throw in a couple of vague plans, and there it would be. But if you want to lay a foundation able to withstand all of the tidal forces of the religions of the world, tough homework is needed. Personally, I feel profound gratitude to Dee Hock for making sure that we are not half-baked, but solidly structured for the future. David Cooperrider and his Appreciative Inquiry and Dee Hock and his Chaordic Alliance provided URI with partnerships that were essential to URI's existence and success.

Meanwhile, during the years that we were working with Dee, I kept circling the world, seeking support, responding to inquiries, and growing a presence for URI.

In 1997, the Archbishop of Canterbury had asked me to represent him for an international interfaith prayer service sponsored by the Tendai Buddhists on Mt. Hiei, Japan. And later on, in 1998, I returned to Japan to be the keynote speaker at the Thirtieth Anniversary of the Japan Religious Committee for the World Federation in Kyoto. I said, "If there is ever going to be a United Religions, it will only happen because the Ultimate Ground of Being wills it to happen. Doors will open and paths will clear away roadblocks if the Divine Spirit has a common vocation for religions working in concert."

Another journey took me to the Lambeth Conference of the Anglican Communion in Canterbury, England. All of the Anglican bishops of the world meet every ten years, and 1998 was the year. On that occasion, the bishops all gather for a composite picture. I was the only bishop not present for the photo. I couldn't make it for the picture because I had to be in London to give the Francis Younghusband Lecture to the members of The World Congress of Faiths. Sir Sigmund Sternberg, a notable international interfaith leader, was in charge of the evening of the Younghusband Lecture.

My first point in the lecture was that a United Religions is "unthinkable" because of ancient feuds among religions that foster hostilities that sear human hearts at unfathomable depths.

My second point was that conditions which would make a United Religions "think-able" would be a time when interfaith collaborations would become necessary, when religions themselves made interfaith a high priority, and when the secular climate would be ready for it. Since those things were happening, at least a United Religions would be "think-able."

My third point was that a United Religions would be "do-able" if the people who were ushering the idea forward were trustworthy, and if everyone at the table could hold two thoughts at one time, namely, both the integrity of one's own tradition and the integrity of the religions of others.

And my fourth point was that a United Religions is "inevitable." I said: "The United Religions will be inevitable when the world has run out of options. I remember listening to a weary leader of the Middle East say, 'We've tried everything. The only thing we haven't tried yet is peace.' As Northern Ireland is teaching the world, peace is hard and requires vision, courage, sanity, and tenacity. There will never be a United Religions founded on the avoidance of reality. The only reason that a United Religions is inevitable is that the world will demand it—it will happen with or without us because it is inevitable."

I made two quick trips to Europe in 1998. One was to participate in a "Prayer for Peace" outdoor service in Bucharest, Romania with 40,000 people. I wrote this prayer: "O Eternal One, whom we know and worship at a great distance, help us to know you not only as adults through doctrine and liturgy, but also to know you as children do. In full trust may we run to you, seek your embrace, enjoy your presence, rest in your strength, and be lovingly aware of all the other children who draw life from your love. This we pray in the Name of the One who took little children in His arms and blessed them, Jesus Christ our Lord. Amen."

The other European trip in 1998 was a last-minute invitation to speak at a high-powered gathering of the Forward Studies Unit of the European Commission in Brussels, Belgium. The conference was held in the context of the new European Union, and attempted to focus on significant issues that would be facing a united Europe. I gave my standard URI speech and got a wide and wild variety of comments. "Naive." "Infantile." "Best presentation of the conference."

Here is a sampling of ideas and thoughts that floated around at that conference:

Change the name "United Religions" and take a Maori word like Su-mage (phonetic spelling), which means a family going in a canoe on a long journey together.

If religions do come together, it will create power to influence the politics of the world. What is the UR policy on international political power? Or, could it potentially create a power to unite religions against non-believers—a crusade.

An interfaith group climbed Mt. Sinai and the only thing they could think to do together without being intrusive was to hum. Maybe silence is the only practical form of common interfaith worship.

Be cautious of an essay treatment of URI. Have a Charter that sings. He lamented that the world is up to here in wordy, irrelevant charters.

Comic relief—URI could be seen as a pharmacy with pioneers getting each religion in a pill. If you are too busy, take a Zen Buddhist pill. If your morals are shaky, take ten Jewish tablets. If you are feeling absent-minded, take a Christian incarnation pill. After every interfaith conference, have your stomach pumped.

The voice of suffering is the litmus test for religion recovering its human dimension. Religion can lose its humanity. Religion has to reinterpret its mission, because proselytizing will never allow a United Religions to exist.

United Religions must not become a bouquet. The flowers of a bouquet are cut from their roots to make a thing of beauty that lasts for only a very short time. Instead, United Religions must be tended as a garden, one that is constantly cultivated, so that a rooted beauty may appear and endure.

The United Religions Charter cannot be the rock upon which everything is built. It has to be the starting point for an evolutionary journey. Thus, a capacity for reformation must be built into it.

One of the most intriguing calls came from the son-in-law of the president of the Church of Latter Day Saints, the head of the Mormons. He told me that in planning for the Winter Olympics of 2002, the Mormons did not want to be seen as using this event for purposes of evangelism. They didn't want to be seen as putting on a Mormon Olympics: they wanted it to be an interfaith Olympics. Would I fly to Salt Lake City and work on this?

Yes I would. On my first of several trips, I was floored to discover that Salt Lake City was not an exclusively Mormon city. Fifty percent of the residents were Jews, Buddhist, Muslims, Christians, and others. I visited various houses of worship and got to know the religious leaders. We started an interfaith luncheon roundtable where we sorted out the issues and made plans. We were so successful that we became an interfaith model for future Olympics. The interfaith roundtables succeeded on another dimension also: thirteen years later, they were still meeting to discuss mutual interests, becoming a forum for ongoing local interfaith dialogue.

Those were days of yeasty confrontations, of frequent flyer miles earned and spent, of planting seeds, of learning from Visa and from the religious histories of nations. And all the while, I kept on performing all of my duties as the bishop of a large and complicated diocese. The two key strategic partnerships formed with David Cooperrider and Dee Hock saved URI—and me—from one-dimensional solutions to many-faceted problems. It was thrilling!

In one more effort at growing a presence, in 1998 I wrote a book entitled *The Coming United Religions*. It contained two important sources. First, Archbishop Desmond Tutu said in the book's Foreword, "Our home is heaven where God is. On earth we learn how to discover home, and each faith leads its adherents homeward. We must learn here how to live together with those with whom we will spend eternity. How can we arrogantly claim that ours is the only way and not learn to remove our shoes as we stand on what others consider to be holy ground, where they catch their glimpse of the Eternal, the Inscrutable, the Holy, the Compassionate, the Gracious One? May the Initiative described in this book succeed for the sake of all believers."

Second, Marcus Braybrooke created a historical chart of proposals for a United Religions from 1893 to 1996. In his brief and incomplete history, he ended with my own efforts to create a United Religions. This chart is available in the Appendix at the back of this book.

Chapter 19
The Seventy-Two-Hour Event
and the Charter Signing in Pittsburgh

Before the URI Charter was signed in Pittsburgh, in June 2000, and before we were a global network, someone at the 1997 Stanford Summit imagined a great event taking place around the upcoming Millennium moment—when time changed from the twentieth century to the twenty-first century! After much discussion, we agreed that we would focus on the day before the change, the day of the change, and the day after the change. We called it "Seventy-Two Hours." We would challenge people of all faiths to walk together into a new age of peace making. And we would trust them to figure out locally how to do that. It was an audacious concept on a conspicuous occasion, and it would test the power of the URI to mobilize people throughout the world. If we succeeded, then the evidence would be clear that United Religions had not only boldness, but also gravity and reach. We never looked at the possibility of failing. We trusted that the people who attended the Stanford Summits were of sufficient enthusiasm and creativity to pull it off. And they were. Wildly so!

Over a million people in sixty countries participated in seventy-two Hours. There was a first-ever peace march of Muslims, Christians, Baha'i, Sikhs, Hindus, and Parsi from Karachi, Pakistan to the Khyber Pass. There was a seventy-two–hour prayer vigil in Malta. People from twenty-five religions celebrated together atop Corcovado in Rio de Janeiro. There was a peace vigil by the prison inmates on death row in San Quentin Prison. And it went on and on. URI was launched. If we could do this, I thought, we could certainly get the UR up and running in June of the Millennium year.

Personally, I took part in a street march in California that started at a Methodist Church in Oakland and ended up at a Buddhist Monastery in Berkeley. On that occasion, I said:

"Never worry about starting out small—the idea that Buddhists and Methodists can make peace—this reality will inspire Hindus and Sikhs, Muslims and Jews to make the same discovery. Small or large isn't the real measure. The real measure is how sincere your heart is. The old century of never looking past your borders is over. Those old walls have to come down, and we must now find the people behind the walls. We must build our new world on mutual respect, harmony, and the happiness we feel today."

Pittsburgh, Pennsylvania! Why in the world would we think of signing the Charter of the United Religions Initiative in Pittsburgh, of all places? That question was asked often and with great feeling. The answer was three-fold.

First, it was symbolic. Pittsburgh is the city of bridges. Bridges rise over the Monongahela River, the Allegheny River, and their confluence in the Ohio River. And all of the bridges are within the city limits of Pittsburgh. If the first and foremost principle of URI is that it is a bridge-building organization and not a religion, why shouldn't we go to the bridge city and sign our Charter there, and picture our Charter and our community with a background of bridges.

Second, it was personal. When my father had a heart attack and had to stop being a golf pro, he went to work for the Pittsburgh Press as a circulation man in the lower Ohio Valley. So we would often go to Pittsburgh, the big town that fascinated our family. Later on, when I was in college, I went to Pittsburgh during the summer to make money for my education. For a while I worked in a glue factory labeling cans with the new glue product. Afterwards, I got a job as a breakdown man on a loading dock in Pittsburgh. During the night shift, I was the only worker who had not served time in the state penitentiary. Still later, when Mary and I lived in West Virginia towns outside of Pittsburgh, our big treat was to go there for celebratory family events. Pittsburgh was a big deal for us.

Third, it was financial. I knew that the Charter-signing event was going to cost a lot of money, and raising that money would be ninety-five percent my responsibility. I couldn't think of another city in the world, apart from San Francisco, where I would have a chance of raising the money—except Pittsburgh. I did have some affluent connections with banks, foundations, and individuals. So I lobbied for the signing to take place in a place that could be counted on to come up with some, if not all, of the needed money.

Goethe is often given credit for writing these words: "… [T]he moment one definitely commits oneself, then Providence moves too. All sorts of things occur to help one that would never otherwise have occurred. A whole stream of events issues from the decision, raising in one's favor all manner of unforeseen incidents and meetings and material assistance, which no man could have dreamed would have come his way." I found this to be remarkably so, as all of the URI people pointed our faces toward Pittsburgh, Pennsylvania and the signing of the Charter on June 26, 2000.

Here are a couple of examples. Mary and I were $800,000 in debt on the million-dollar line of credit, which we took out to start the United Religions. Then one hot August morning, while lots of people were on vacation, a handful of us were in the office working on the Charter. The phone rang. One member of the staff ran down the hall to answer and soon returned. "Who was it?" we asked. It was a lady whose mother had died in Germany and left her some money to give away immediately. The lady had called all sorts of organizations trying to give the money away and was always met by the following response: "Our Development Director is on an August vacation. Call back in September." We paused. Then I got on the phone and told her that we were in business in August and would gladly receive her gift. I said, "Well, we're here. And we're ready to go." Three days later a check for a million dollars arrived.

Here's another instance. A dear friend of mine who had been married several times wanted to marry again. I promised that I would do the wedding—on two conditions. First it had to take place on the Island of Iona in the Inner Hebrides of Scotland, and second, my wife, Mary and I would have to go on their honeymoon to get them started right (and to play a little golf). So, on the Island of Iona I ran into an outrageous English priest who was leading a retreat for elders. We made him the flower girl at the wedding. Afterwards, as I went down to the ferry landing, readying for a small boat to carry us to the Isle of Mull, I sat on the grass and the English priest appeared. I casually told him that I was starting the United Religions. Next thing I knew, we had a URI Conference at Windsor Castle, and in 2000, we had an English signing of the URI Charter in the Millennium Dome in London amid grand fanfare. URI-UK was launched at the ferry landing on Iona by happenstance, and then was launched in London by design.

The pace was quickening for me. The signing of the Charter in Pittsburgh was coming fast, and I was traveling far. At St.

George's Cathedral in Cape Town, South Africa I preached about the call to repentance by John the Baptist. I could imagine him saying:

1. Each religion must face the reality check of violence, which is at the core of its story and history. For instance, in the Judeo-Christian tradition people have learned that God loves them because we were successful in slaughtering people of other religions.

2. Religions cannot keep competing against each other trying to win superiority by having more babies than their religious competitors. Life is becoming intolerable and the planet unsustainable as the major religions try to win a global birth contest in the name of evangelism.

3. Religions cannot hide behind the covert strategy of gentle conversion while in truth using every economic and cultural intimidation as well as threat of physical violence in order to gain conversions and conquest over other faiths. "Today there are men, women and children all over the world who yearn for religions to go back to their deepest stories to see if there is any room for people of other religions."

In Jerusalem His Holiness, the Dalai Lama, Dick Blum, and I held an Interfaith Conference in June 1999. And my main learning was that little comes from having the "big names" posturing. Yes, it was a memorable experience for many and for me. Yes, it did some good as a symbolic gesture. But it didn't scratch the surface of the real life of people who live there. The one funny moment came when I was put on a panel with a local Muslim leader called Imam Sway. I said that back in the 1940s, I would listen to a popular bandleader who was always introduced with these words: "Swing and

Sway with Sammy Kaye." Never did I imagine that fifty years later in Jerusalem Swing and Sway would be on a panel together.

After a mad-dash speaking tour on the East Coast and the South of the United States, I ended up in Pittsburgh to raise money and to meet with the local contingent who were working out the details of the Charter signing. One last thought occurred to me: why not visit Mr. Fred Rogers, the most popular children's TV host of *Mr. Roger's Neighborhood?*

Children all over America adored this joyfully openhearted, kind gentleman. He broadcast from Pittsburgh and introduced children to children of other races and cultures and backgrounds. It seemed natural that Mr. Rogers, a Presbyterian minister who created an accepting neighborhood where every child was appreciated, would want to do a show that makes it okay to meet children of other religions in his neighborhood. I met with him and to my utter dismay he didn't want to do a show that had anything to do with religion or children of other religions. That made no sense to me. Fred was an ordained Presbyterian minister, so religion was not foreign to him. His entire fame was based on accepting different people in the neighborhood. Why he refused to embrace the differences of religions is a complete mystery to me.

What did that say to me? It said that religions have invested so much energy into demeaning other religions that anyone who would dare attempt to break the cycle of mutual contempt would be vulnerable to harsh criticism and fierce retribution. In many cases, children have been taught that the people of other religions are monsters. Even Mr. Rogers was unwilling to unmask the monsters and allow children to discover the humanity behind the costume. So I concluded that the interfaith movement at the end of the twentieth century was up against subterranean, dark forces of resistance and potential vengeance. Surface interfaith victories might sprout up occasionally, but the real challenge would have to be played out in invisible realms where the soul wrestles with monsters and imagines the bliss of religious genocide. The scene with Mr. Rogers shook me.

By the way, lots of people in Pittsburgh found our upcoming Charter Signing to be repugnant. The local Episcopal bishop, my colleague, said that peace among religions was too hot to handle. He worked to keep Episcopalians away from the event. The Roman Catholic bishop was worse. He told his clergy that Swing was out to make one religion out of all of the religions and place himself at the top of it. And this came after we had a conversation during which I pointed out that URI's first principle is that we are not a religion but a bridge-building organization. He and his folks boycotted us as well. There were lots of dynamics of religious politics at play. Thank goodness for the local Jews, Presbyterians, Hindus, Muslims, Jains, and others who rallied behind us, working hard to make it a success.

Initially, my idea of a United Religions had created a stir in the world of religion. Not a major earthquake, but enough of a jolt to warrant a conversation among religious leaders, to arouse suspicion and animosity among critics (two books were published quickly about my villainy in proposing such syncretism and universalism), and enough to inspire grass-roots believers of many persuasions to throw in their hats with us. After my hard talk with Professor Hans Kung in Tubingen, Germany in 1996, I was willing to set aside for a while my inspiration for a United Religions, and to make my temporary peace with the necessity of a United Religions Initiative. This made for a certain amount of imprecision. Sometimes I mentioned "UR" sometimes I called the same thing "URI." Clearly I was bouncing around with what to do with my vision and my vow to start a United Religions.

My compromise was that we would have an Initiative until June 26, 2000. Then it would become the real thing, the United Religions. But no matter how I tried to straddle the chasm, it didn't work. Coming back on a plane from Japan one night, I wrote: "It is clearer and clearer that the URI has to aspire to the greatest comprehensive interfaith network possible. That means we must immediately, after signing the Charter, put primary creative energy into the development of a foundational support institute that would cover global communication, education, training, research, fundraising, youth corps, humanitarian responses to crisis, et al. Without the full institution, the URI will evolve into just one more international interfaith organization." A foundational support institution! What in the world would that be? It was my last desperate attempt to hold on to the dream that launched me on this quest.

All along, we organizers talked about having an Initiative that would be the scaffolding upon which we would stand to create a United Religions. But as the big day of charter-signing approached, this all seemed hollow. We saw the grandiosity of religious groups in naming themselves. "The World Council of Churches" does not include the Roman Catholics or Pentecostals. If they are not at the table as full-fledged members, how can this be a world council of churches? And the Roman Catholic Church refers to itself as "Catholic," meaning universal, while there is lots of Christianity outside the universe of Rome. And so on. The last thing that we wanted to do was to refer to ourselves as "The United Religions" when we knew full well that we did not have a buy-in from all of the religions. So instead of going from a United Religions Initiative to a United Religions, we went from a vision of a United Religions to a very practical United Religions Initiative.

Did that hurt? Yes. Along the way, it was made abundantly clear to me that a UR would not happen at this time, on my watch. This sadness was certainly offset by the thousands and thousands of people who leapt in to inaugurate the URI. Besides, "United Religions" was still in our name. At the same time, it is a name that is off-putting to some because it mirrors the United Nations, or because it seems to imply that we have corralled all of the religions into our domain.

When I went around the world in 1996, I had a postcard to give away. On one side was a photo taken from the Hubble Telescope of the birth of a star. The words on this side read: "The world is waiting for the birth of new light...the United Religions Initiative." Then on the other side, is an invitation to enter into a sacred trust, to join in prayer and meditation to prepare for the coming of a United Religions, which will change the world. Today I am that postcard. Out in front of me is the URI, but on the other side of my heart lives a sacred trust for the eventual creation of a United Religions that will change the world.

On June 26, 2000, a dream died for all practical purposes. And on that day a star was born. May the star shine brightly and may the dream endure as a seed in the ground that one day in the future will blossom and change the world. Ironically, in my pursuit of a United Religions, I had missed on the vision. I had completely missed on the response of religious leaders. I had entirely missed on the timing of events. And I totally missed on the planning that would make it happen. Nevertheless, though I flayed away blindly, I actually hit a home run. On the wall of my study is a saying by the great home-run hitter, Babe Ruth. He said, "You can't hit 'em if you don't SWING at 'em." That makes sense to me. As the years have gone by since then, I can see little signs that the world is still moving toward a United Religions, even if such an entity has little to do with the way I had imagined it. The interconnecting chords of necessity, affection, scholarship, interfaith experience, and technology seem to be braiding a weave of uncommon thread. Not on my watch, but a United Religions is on its way.

Meanwhile, what actually happened in Pittsburgh? That story is brilliantly told in Charles Gibbs' and Sally Mahé's book, *Birth of a Global Community: Appreciative Inquiry in Action.* If I close my eyes and think of the Pittsburgh signing, here is what I see: drummers; a Jesuit crying in a field; dancing on a mountain overlooking the Gold Gate Triangle; valiant local people displaying religious and cultural food, costumes and music; events at Carnegie Mellon University and the University of Pittsburgh that far exceeded my highest hopes; sitting outside in an Italian Restaurant and watching the URI world walk by as naturally as sunrise; seeing Dick Blum walk through the door to sign the Charter after having flown the length of the country at the last minute. And seeing the Charter on a table in front of me—at last—and then kissing it.

Chapter 20
The Young Toddler Begins To Walk Globally:
URI at Age One

In Pittsburgh, lots of people extended invitations to Charles Gibbs and me to see the remarkable work that URI had begun in their regions. There were so many countries to visit, and because of my duties as a bishop, so little time. But we settled on Sri Lanka, India, and Pakistan for March 2001. Since URI was less than a year old, we didn't expect to see much progress. We figured that most of the trip would be about promotion, hoping for future growth. But our eyes were opened. Out in the world, URI was spreading beyond our imagining.

This muscular journey was hampered by health issues. An earlier cold had turned into a full-blown case of viral pneumonia months before I began the trip. Coughing all day and night, with a neck frozen stiff, I went to my doctor to ask if it would be wise to make this trip. He said that viral pneumonia had to run its course no matter where I was. So it would be okay to cough in Sri Lanka as well as San Francisco. That was all I needed to hear. Charles and I took off.

The first surprise was in Singapore, where we stopped for a day to change planes. URI folks in the region made sure that we were met by some of their friends, a CEO of an internet company and his lawyer wife. After a great meal and exploring how URI could take root there, we had an appointment with a famous radio personality, hoping to get good coverage for URI. We anticipated that a URI regional meeting could be held in Singapore in the future. This was our first hint that an international network was spontaneously forming. It was pretty heady stuff for two guys from the office in San Francisco who had no Singapore expectations.

After a short flight to Sri Lanka, our eyes grew wider. We were treated with great honor by the largest safety-net organization in the country, the Sarvodaya Shanthi Sena Sansadaya movement. They were amazing people who work in thousands of locales and provide essential services to all of the communities. For instance, Charles and I visited a nursery for orphans who had been abandoned on the streets, a vocational class of developmentally disabled people, and a large drug and alcohol rehabilitation group, which had become URI's second Cooperation Circle in this nation.

My position as an Episcopal bishop came in handy for me here, as it did in many places around the world. First of all, the Episcopal connection got us into the home of the Anglican vicar, the Rev. Prince Devananda, who was Singhalese and whose wife was Tamil. Here, we got real-life stories of how great a price can be paid with interracial, intercultural marriages. Both of their parents refused to attend their wedding. Due to my Episcopal connection, the Anglican bishop of the Diocese of Colombo (the capital of Sri Lanka), invited us to a long and instructive breakfast before worship services at his cathedral. The bishop, Kenneth Fernando, had been a key figure in peace negotiations between the leaders of the Tamil Tigers (LTTE) and the Singhalese leaders. Kenneth made many dangerous journeys back and forth from the capital to the jungle headquarters of the Tamil during the twelve-year civil war, carrying the terms of a peace negotiation.

Kenneth was part of a first wave of interfaith leaders in Sri Lanka who had spent decades learning about other faiths

(his Ph.D. was in The Buddhist Tradition), forging relationships across religious borders, and entering into dialogues.
Now, this first wave of leaders was becoming a gray-haired
group, while a new wave was coming along looking for actions beyond dialogue, and wanting to be independent of
the backing of great religions or existing international interfaith groups. When they saw that URI was basically net-
working existing efforts, and linking people globally
without tampering excessively with local autonomy, they
were extremely responsive to Charles and me. We were tap-
ping into fresh vitality that was beyond our fondest hopes.

Then, the saddest of sad news arrived. An email told us
that Dawson Wambi, a rising star of URI in Africa, was
dead. He had stayed late at a URI meeting in one village
and had to drive a long way to be an election observer in
another village. Driving too fast along the way, he was surprised by a youngster who darted into his path. Trying to
avoid hitting the boy, Dawson swerved his car. Too late; he
killed the boy, and on the opposite side of the road his ca-
reening car killed three more boys. An angry crowd
grabbed him, stoned him, and cut off his legs and head.
Horror upon horror upon horrors.

This news came as I left the airport in Colombo to journey
to New Delhi, India. Charles stayed on in Sri Lanka to explore the possibilities of holding URI gatherings there. Getting off the airplane, I expected to take a cab to my
destination. Instead, a delegation of faith and interfaith leaders met me. It was the beginning of scenes that are forever
etched into my memory.

First was a visit to the Rohini Self-Help Project. I must admit
to being a little squeamish about surface cleanliness. But

here I was in a sprawling slum. In the streets, flies swarmed over dung, over rotten food, over pools of polluted water and over abject poverty and emaciated people. On the other hand, the people were upbeat and positive. An outdoor class of school children was well attended by eager faces. A fabulous woman doctor, and mostly Sikh representatives of a Youth Corps, provided quality leadership.

Someone went to a local faucet and brought me a glass of water. Oh my, what to do? I immediately took a walk rather than a sip. With a host of bright young youth leaders, I toured the entire project. Upon my return, I was presented with a large plate of food. Oh my, here we go again. I asked for a Coca-Cola and picked carefully through the plate.

After a breathtaking schedule of meetings, Charles and I went to a public school, the Salwan Public School. We were thinking that it would be polite and promising like our other appointments, but this was far beyond that. There were hundreds and hundreds of well-dressed people to greet us; while we, on the other hand, were in our khakis and no jackets. Our names were on a large sign of welcome in front of this very affluent school. Flowers littered our path for hundreds of yards. Signs of URI were everywhere. The seven thousand students of Salwan Public School had become a URI Cooperation Circle. Then we had a meeting around a large sunken stage on a beautiful night. After speeches, the students sang, "We Are The Children." Children aged five to eight gave a truly marvelous performance of an original musical allegory all about tolerance and restoration coming from the pursuit of harmony. Then came another performance—of great dancing and costumes—with some Michael Jackson music, no less. The master of ceremonies said that there is only one God and one human family. Perhaps this will become a one-sentence description of the foundational theology that URI inspires.

The next morning, March 21, was Mary's birthday, and here I was in New Delhi heading for a rock quarry. That morning, Charles and I were picked up by the greatly revered and sometimes feared Swami Agnivesh. What an amazing and effective man he is. Originally, he was a lawyer and a teacher before becoming a Hindu Swami. Then he stopped worshipping Hindu idols and poured himself into social justice. On our way out of town, we stopped at a red light, and the driver of the car on my right spotted the Swami, jumped out of the car, bowed to him while nodding a Namaste gesture of greeting, and then drove away. Everywhere we went that day, people knelt on the ground to touch his feet, or the hem of his robe. He would always recoil and say, "Stop it." He abhors idolatry, especially when he is the subject of adulation.

We drove to a rocky countryside where indentured people—children, women, and men—were reducing large rocks to tiny stones. They were slaves because their parents or grandparents had run up debts at the "company store" which they could not pay back. So they and all their generations thereafter were indentured to pay off the debt. It is against the law; nevertheless it is a frequent practice. Swami helped some of them go free, and for the others, he started a union to raise their wages and improve their living conditions. Of course the leaders of the company store countered this by trying to kill Swami Agnivesh and his colleagues on the highways in crashes between quarry trucks and little automobiles. As a matter of fact, we visited at the home of one of the widows of these road murders. Then we went to the quarry itself, as well as to school classes, and even the company store. In all of these places, I kept wondering what better impact could be achieved if people of different religions got together to improve the plight of the slaves rather than leaving it all to a designated saint and agitator.

That evening, back in New Delhi, Charles and I began an ongoing sojourn with a remarkable leader of the International Society for Krishna Consciousness (ISKCON), Dr. T. D. Singh. T. D. earned a Ph.D. in Chemistry, had a superb singing voice, and instantly threw himself into URI. His backing was no small thing in India. Many doors flew open to us in welcome. That night, we jumped into a cab and plunged into horrendous traffic with a teenage Kamikaze-type driver. Of course, I was in the front seat where my prayer life improved as my demise beckoned. The air conditioner was blasting, the Delhi air pollution (the world's worst) was seizing my lungs, and I so wished that I were home celebrating Mary's birthday. Before this trip, all I knew about the Hare Krishnas was what I had learned in airports from disciples handing out flowers and dancing around. My education deepened quickly as we entered one of their temples, which was full of worshippers, twenty-four hours a day. As we went up the stairs of the temple, around 1:00 a.m., people fell to the ground at the sight of Dr. T. D. Singh. They lay prostrate, touching his feet. Charles and I realized that we were in for an education and an adventure.

The next day, we flew with T. D. Singh to the city of Imphal, in the State of Manipur, which is east and north of Bangladesh. It is really remote. As we entered the town, we saw a large URI banner over the main street. At a press conference, one member of the local URI Cooperation Circle got up and recited from memory the entire Charter of URI—Preamble, Purpose and twenty-one Principles. Heavens, I couldn't do that. We had come a long way from home to see if URI had taken root in the world. We had a resounding answer yes, in an unlikely place.

On our big day there we were to start early in the morning and pay official visits to six religious sites, accompanied by two or three hundred people of several differing faiths. People of the Sikh Gurdwara Temple got up at 2:30 a.m. to pray for the success of this day. Thinking that our stay at the temple was merely going to last twenty minutes, I sat on the floor and crossed my legs like everyone else. An hour and a half later I got up—with lots of help from Charles. My 57-year-old knees were locked immobile.

Next, we went to a Jain Temple to revere Lord Mahavir, who founded Jainism 2600 years ago. As expected of visitors to the temple, I sat on the floor cross-legged, suffering more knee misery. Asked to speak, I again couldn't move. Charles had to get me up and prop me against a wall so I could give my speech. At the next stop, Charles pulled me down the street to the Muslim Mosque Masjid Hatta, where friendly Muslims had us sit cross-legged (again) and pray on their porch. Happily, our marathon through the faiths of Imphal led us next to a holy site, Kangla Laipham, of the indigenous people of that land. Chairs were provided. Ah, what a relief.

Then we went on to the Roman Catholic cathedral, and later to the Krishna temple—at both places we were invited to sit in chairs, so things were looking up. Hundreds of people made all six stops with us, and most of them said that they had lived here all of their lives and had never stepped inside anyone else's house of worship.

The day ended in a very large convocation with the Chief Minister (governor) of the state of Manipur. The governor, Charles, T.D. Singh, and I were surrounded by people with heavy weapons, protecting us in case insurgents made an attack. What we learned was that in the nearby hill country, Roman Catholics of the Naga tribe and the Baptists of the Kuki tribe had been engaged in ethnic cleansing. The core fight was about tribal lands, boundaries, rent, collections, vindication, and the constant threat of eighteen different insurgent groups. Hard questions arose from the audience at the convocation about what URI might have to say or do about this horrendous situation. Charles and I did our best. At the end, the chief minister of Manipur gave an eloquent and moving speech. He told about taking office and not wanting government soldiers killing the insurgents. "They are our daughters and sons," he said. So he declared an immediate truce and said that he saw that URI had the potential to be an agent of making peace among the warring religions. He gave us his wholehearted endorsement, stating that URI was exactly what Manipur and India needs right now.

Our leave-taking on the next day at the Imphal Airport provided a change of pace. Charles, T. D., and I started walking across the tarmac toward our plane in a torrential downpour, all of us with umbrellas. Once on the plane, the three of us were seated in the first row opposite the open door. As soon as we were seated, a deluge of water came through the door and onto us, while the flight attendants ran for cover. Then came large chunks of hail through the door that bounced off our faces. All three of us grabbed our umbrellas again and hunkered down, sheltered behind them on the plane, laughing hysterically.

After a series of meetings in Mumbai, T. D. left for his office in Calcutta while Charles and I headed for Lahore, Pakistan. We had some staunch allies there, and chief among them was Father James Channan, who had attended most of URI's formative sessions at Stanford University, and Dr. Javid Iqbal, who was a key presence at our first Youth Conference in 1995 and host to Mary and me when we first traveled to introduce United Religions in 1996. More important, Javid was the son of the original spiritual giant of Pakistan, Muhammad Iqbal, and Javid was not only a member of the Supreme Court of Pakistan but also a Senator. When our plane touched down, a sizeable crowd bedecked us with garlands of so many roses that I felt as though I had just won the Kentucky Derby.

Pakistan was not all flowers though. One influential man who had just made his Hajj in Mecca published a fairly long treatise attacking URI as being anti-Muslim. His words were translated into eighty-three languages and circulated around the world. I heard about him many times in this Muslim country of Pakistan.

Charles and I had planned for three full days in Lahore, the main cultural center of Pakistan, and then a return trip home. But it didn't turn out quite like that.

The first day in Lahore found us at a news conference, a book launching, and a tour of a new building dedicated to Muhammad Iqbal. Then we made a visit to the Badshahi Mosque, which holds 100,000 people for its worship services. We met the aged imam of the mosque who had become an interfaith leader after Jesus appeared to him one night in his sleep. Later on his son, Maulana Abdul Qadir Azad, not only became the new imam but also a member of URI's

Global Council. Since this mosque is the national mosque of Pakistan, it means a great deal that its leaders are connected to URI. Oddly enough, we ended this day at a Rotary Club Center where a URI man and his wife were opening a restaurant. Charles and I gave speeches. Then we went back to the Dominican Center, where we were staying with Father James for the night.

Reflecting on all of the Cooperation Circles popping up in Pakistan, it dawned on me that all over the world people of different faiths are beginning to realize that something quite significant is unresolved when religions have to deal with each other. All of us have been taught about the uniqueness of each of our faiths, but we have not learned how to live fairly and charitably with people of other faiths. Cooperation Circles are tiny experiments in the long march toward resolving the problems caused by people of differing faiths who have to live side by side. Cooperation Circles are humble beginnings in learning to coexist with the help of inter-religious hospitality and common actions.

The second day in Lahore was a prime lesson in coming to know that events in Pakistan never start on time—or end anywhere near the planned time. Case in point: We went to an international conference at the Pakistan Workers Trust for a 10:00 a.m. start. But nothing happened until 11:00 a.m. After a few formalities, it was time for open mike. For the next three hours the speeches were interminable and rude and most of the people attending left midcourse. Yet the remaining audience loved it. I was the keynote speaker, and because the time was almost 2:00 p.m., I was told to keep my remarks to no more than five minutes. Fine with me!

Then, quite an amazing thing happened. We were met at the offices of a leading newspaper by the Rt. Rev. Andrew Francis, the tall, handsome, poised, intelligent Roman Catholic bishop of Multan. Because he was tied tightly to the Vatican and because the Vatican was not keen on me, or URI, I was expecting the worst. I could not have been more wrong. Bishop Francis was generous and most supportive. It was his custom to make public statements in support of URI throughout the world. He said that it doesn't matter if Christianity is a minority or a majority religion in Pakistan; what matters is the healing power of Jesus Christ's Spirit, which is the Holy Spirit. In the power of the Spirit, the Church could participate with all of the religions in the URI.

A 3:30 p.m. lunch almost happened. Back at the Dominican Center, I was just about to take a bite of my sandwich when through the door came a reporter from Pakistan's largest newspaper, The Dawn. For the first half hour we talked about his family and his work in Dubai. For the next half hour, he interviewed me. And for the last half hour, he told me his answers to the questions he had just asked me.

When that was over, I stepped outside, exhausted, and hoped to have a moment to myself. But no such luck. Just then, fifteen men from different Cooperation Circles around Pakistan spotted me and wanted to sit down at once and have a meeting. So we went back inside, and upstairs, where there was a room full of people of different Cooperation Circles who wanted to be heard.

At that point, Charles Gibbs, who had been packing to go back to San Francisco early due to a family emergency, bid us all adieu. Not only had it been fun to travel with Charles, but also, on so many occasions when I had reached my level of incompetence, I simply turned to Charles who articulately and invariably came up with remote details that were oh, so relevant.

What I heard from the different Cooperation Circles touched my heart. For instance, one Muslim said that he lived in Karachi, the "killing capital" of Pakistan, and he found the URI to be a new model for Muslims in his country. Of course he added that he had to sacrifice his prestige in the Muslim community to be involved with URI. Another person added that once he had read the URI Charter, he discovered that it was much more sophisticated than anything he had ever read in the interfaith world, so he signed on. Beyond these comments was an evening full of similar testimonies that opened my eyes to how deeply URI had penetrated the hearts and minds of the people in this country.

Senator Javid Iqbal and Father James Channan hosted a spectacular dinner in the front yard of the Dominican Center, with golden carpets hanging from wires. The whole scene resembled a banquet fit for Bedouin royalty. At 10:30 p.m., I finally got something to eat—a feast, no less. Afterwards, I was so looking forward to sleep—but two more meetings were arranged for me.

The next morning, the supposed last day of the journey, brought a day that tipped my poor viral-pneumonia-infected body over the edge. We drove to Youhanabad, Pakistan, to a school that was heavily supported by URI. A carpet rolled out for us with rose petals in our path. Then, we walked to a lane where children, indentured to a company that made Nike-like shoes, earned $1 a month. We saw absolutely filthy streets with no sewer system and new garbage piled on old garbage. Nevertheless, the people were upbeat whenever we stopped in to chat in people's houses that doubled as miniature tennis shoe factories as well as living quarters. Then, we drove past buffaloes bathing in dark pools to a school where all of the children sang, "Baa, Baa, Black Sheep, Have You Any Wool?" We had a good laugh.

We arrived in another village where a tent had been set up for a URI event. Then it happened. The pneumonia that had been dissipating got stirred up again. Dancing children greeted us and led us to the front row. For five hours I had to sit there with a large fan blowing in my face. I had not eaten lunch. The absolute worst speaker was a former army officer who claimed to be a bishop in Rev. Moon's Unification Church. He preached a remarkably inept sermon three times in three different languages. Finally, he was bribed to quit preaching with the promise that he could preach next time there was such a gathering. Other such demagoguery followed his fifty-minute oration. The good parts of the event involved an ethnic dance by young girls, an original play about mothers-in-law, and the sight of little URI flags flying in all directions. Through it all, I could feel a rising cold rekindling the fading pneumonia. I hoped that this URI event served as a character-builder.

Although it was late afternoon, I was persuaded by our hosts to drive off to yet another area to meet people of a new URI Cooperation Circle. While en route, a grand windstorm blew ferociously, and a colossal rainstorm followed. After stopping to ask for directions at least fifteen times, we arrived at dusk in the back streets of Mahmood Buti, a poor Muslim village. We got out of the car in the rain and discovered that the little crowd in front of a store was our crowd. We were taken down a narrow alley and plunked in a small room full of furniture. Someone offered me a Coke at 6:30

p.m.; my first sustenance since 6:30 a.m. Then, we were led through the dark to a porch where seventy-five people were sitting. Quickly, I realized that these people had never heard of the URI and were as surprised to see me as I was to see them. They had shown up because they were told that someone from an NGO was in town, and that meant that they might get some money. Yes, URI is indeed an NGO (Non-Governmental Organization), but we have no money to distribute to Cooperation Circles. Ours is a ninety-nine percent volunteer organization, where each Cooperation Circle is self-funding.

The good news is that the longer we talked, the more they warmed up to the idea of a URI. At the end, they walked me to the car and gave me an embrace. It was an odd encounter that started cynically and ended with an affectionate moment.

After another long drive across Lahore, I arrived at the elegant estate of Bishop Samuel Azariah, the head of the Church of Pakistan. I was wearing my soaking-wet, thin, short-sleeve purple shirt, and then went out to a late, late dinner at a Chinese restaurant that had a cold air-conditioner blowing. Later on, at midnight, as I was staggering toward bed, anticipating a good night's sleep and a return flight to San Francisco in the morning, Father James burst in and said, "I have wonderful news. Tomorrow morning at 9:30 a.m., you are going to be on television in Islamabad. We can get our message out to sixty million viewers." Islamabad was a four-hour drive away. So I packed, set the alarm, and collapsed for a few hours.

Actually, we arrived at the TV station at 9:28 a.m., in time for the show, which went very well. With a change in my airline tickets, I had a few hours in Islamabad, which turned out to be a bonus. It gave me an opportunity to visit a new interfaith university established by a man who showed up once in Salt Lake City, Utah for a URI event just prior to the Winter Olympics in Utah in 2002. When he was spotted taking pictures around the local sights, the FBI arrested him and jailed him for months, fearing that he was part of a plan to terrorize the Olympics. Many conversations followed between the FBI and me. Now in Islamabad, I was interested to see his interfaith university and to get a better sense of what exactly he was up to. It all appeared to be legitimate in Islamabad.

Then, at long last I could return home. The trip had opened my eyes to see how powerfully URI had taken root in Sri Lanka, India, and Pakistan. Clearly, we were a force for good. And clearly, I couldn't keep up the pace of visiting every place. The administration of this effort had to evolve to include multiples of other people. But my stupendous realization was that the mission of URI had touched a deep chord in the hearts of people all over the world, people yearning for religions to be together, to be part of the solution, rather than part of the problem.

I got on the plane in Islamabad and buckled my seatbelt for the first of forty hours of flying that was needed to get me back to San Francisco. My seatmate, a young Pakistani man, asked where I was headed. "The San Francisco Bay Area," I replied. I asked him the same question and he echoed, "The San Francisco Bay Area." He told me that he worked in Silicon Valley, but he and his family lived in Islamabad. Why in the world would he commute 40 hours each way between home and work? He said, "Honestly, I don't want my children exposed to your TV, your music, your movies, your young drug culture. And your almost total disrespect for

Allah. I'd rather pay the price of a long commute than to expose my children to your godless society. I need your money but I am sorry to say to you that I find the way that you all live is morally degenerate." That short exchange sums up a world of Muslim-Christian confrontation.

At midnight on Saturday, I arrived in San Francisco still deeply coughing from viral pneumonia, but that was nothing compared to my fatigue. I got home around 1:30 a.m., slept a few hours, and rose up early to write a sermon for this Sabbath Day. Then I drove to Holy Family Episcopal Church in Half Moon Bay, California, where I preached, celebrated the Sacrament, attended a reception in my honor, and had a working lunch with the Vestry (the local church officials). Mercifully, it was not my typical Sunday routine, when I visited two or three congregations.

I drove home realizing full well that I was living a double life and paying a price. The Episcopal Church didn't care about the United Religions Initiative, and the United Religions Initiative didn't care about the Episcopal Church. But I was providing primary and essential leadership for both. "How long, Lord?" I wondered. Tomorrow I had to get to the office early to address two weeks of work backlog, and the pace would go on.

URI was one year old and prospering. The Episcopal Diocese of California was one hundred and fifty years old and prospering. I felt like I was a thousand years old and running on fumes. Oh, did I mention that I have a wife, two children and three grandchildren?

Chapter 21
The Elastic Dozen Years

My place in the life of URI fluctuated radically in the first twelve official years of this global family, 2001 to 2013. In 2001 it was quite simple. I was the Founder who spent his full time as the bishop of the Episcopal Diocese of California. If I went to the Hub Office or to a Global Assembly, I was greeted as a distant and genuinely welcomed patriarch.

Things changed dramatically when I retired from the Diocese in 2006 and went to work in the URI office. My place was the last room in the building; volunteer secretarial help was available only occasionally; and my job was to be the Assistant to the Development Officer. Major Gifts was my assignment. I quietly attended staff meetings and tried to figure out how I might be of help.

After a couple of years, I suggested that I had connections and gifts that might be of service to URI. Permission was granted me to begin to work with others on a strategic plan for URI. People from outside joined with staff members and me, and for the next four years we labored diligently. What we came up with was a plan to start a President's Council, and to expand our thinking and actions in six critical areas. Each area was to be called a Satellite.

When the Global Council gave me tentative permission to build the plan, I recruited people to work in all of the Satellites, and each one began meeting monthly. Since I presided at all of them, the pace of my involvement increased considerably. Also, I recruited people to be on the President's Council and we met four times a year. It was total immersion for me in the Hub Office, and frankly too much for me to sustain.

Then, a new senior leadership arrangement was made at the URI Hub Office, and I was told to dismantle the Satellites, and I was encouraged to no longer attend staff meetings. In one instance I was told not to speak with a staff member unless I got permission from my superior. But the President's Council was seen as great benefit, so I was allowed to continue with it. I absented myself from the Hub as much as possible and tried to figure out other ways of being of service to URI. The verb "founder" means to sink below the water. Yes, that's what it felt like. Founders can indeed founder. Those four years were, by far, the most difficult and tortuous time in all my experiences with URI. It took all of my buoyancy to stay afloat.

So, I turned my energy to new projects. I experimented with bringing new people into URI by creating a Founder's Circle. I would drive down to Silicon Valley and meet with Hindu and Muslim entrepreneurs, and encourage their participation in URI. I also poured myself into the creation of the Environmental Satellite Cooperation Circle and the Voices for a World Free of Nuclear Weapons Cooperation Circle.

After a retreat of the Environmental Satellite Cooperation Circle, I wrote these words: The organizational design of URI is not based on a hierarchical, Industrial Revolution model of top down. Instead it was based on the way Nature works—biomimicry. What works in a tide pool will work in a Cooperation Circle. That was our leap of faith. This is revolutionary in the world of faith and interfaith. "We have the right to organize in any manner, at any scale, in any area, and around any issue or activity which is relevant to and consistent with the Preamble, Purpose and Principles." Grassroots! URI's very character does not rest on the organizational model of the Roman Empire or General Motors but on Nature. In order for URI to be URI it has to claim its natural foundation. The vocation of our Environmental Cooperation Circle is, in part, to remind us where we came from. And to drive URI's conversations back to basics: "We unite for the benefit of our Earth community." "We unite to heal and protect the Earth." This constitutes our flag in the ground.

URI is not a religion and the environment is certainly not our substitute for religion. Nevertheless, when the people of this Cooperation Circle come together we do honor the disciplines of meditation and silence that the natural order inspires. We haven't made the environment into a religion but we are certainly becoming ever more respectful of the sacred dimension that we intuit in the Earth community.

One highlight experience for me as a leader of the Voices for a World Free of Nuclear Weapons Cooperation Circle was being asked to make a speech at the United Nations in New York, on April 30, 2014, on the occasion of the run-up to the Nuclear Non-Proliferation Treaty (NPT) Convention. I said:

"It would be absurd to imagine in the future an interfaith service after the nuclear holocaust that has already been planned and triggered for this city, for instance. No faiths would be left to collect the mountainous grief. Just a first strike, just a first strike of the weapons that are aimed at us today might annihilate 280 million people. At least that is how many human beings we have targeted today in other parts of the world with our first strike, and I assume there to be some sort of reciprocity of numbers.

"In the face of a catastrophic nuclear Armageddon or the possibility of suitcase bombs or the prospect of rogue states with nuclear designs or individual madness linked with black-market fissile material and all of the retaliations, what has interfaith got to do with these threats? Is the only vocation for interfaith a defensive one after the fact of tragedy, or is there something unique and helpful that the interfaith movement could do up front, beforehand, to challenge the nuclear assumptions that have gotten us to this moment… to humanize the calculation…to prompt believers in God to face up to the abominations that we conspire to commit?

"I would like to submit that the genius of interfaith is its ability to gather together people of a wide range of differing and conflicting persuasions in order to do something creative and deeply needed for the total community. Translated into nuclear disarmament terms, I believe that the interfaith movement could mobilize and energize a far greater team of advocates than now exists…

"We need artists and filmmakers, hip-hoppers and story-tellers. We need to point out that the nuclear issue is THE environmental issue. We need to compete with apocalyptic movies to state that the apocalypse is not entertainment; it is a real threat that needs the good guys to overcome the bad guys. We need to mine the mother lode of stories of nu-clear accidents and close calls and heroes and victims and nuclear greed and insane claims of security and the myth that a super race of people should decide who should be armed and who should be disarmed. We need to tell the whole truth about the financial price being paid and the length of the cleanup, and who will be left holding the dump. We need to heed the scientist telling about 'the Big Bang' of Creation, and face up to our homemade Big Bang that could smash it into destruction. We need to make this issue available to young people, with all of the fear and all of the hope that accompanies nuclear possession and nuclear responsibility."

Then, in the summer of 2013, everything changed. Both members of the senior management team were gone, and the Hub Office was floundering around on its own. I was invited back into the life of the Hub Office by the Global Council, to be an agent of URI's continuity, while everyone readied for URI's second Executive Officer to arrive four months thence. URI 1.0 was over and URI 2.0 was about to begin.

The first twelve years of URI's life found me scrambling around for my identity in this family. It was hard, with hard work, hard emotional swings, hard to stay on course, hard to find the sweet spot where my energy was helpful and not an obstruction. I take pride in making it through the bumpy times and never giving up on my love for URI's vision and people. As I look forward to the continuation of URI 2.0, I must say that I am full of confidence and support for our direction. With the arrival of Victor Kazanjian as URI's second Executive Director, the drift toward command and control in the central office abated; team building and authority sharing were fostered; a return to URI's Charter was accentuated; Cooperation Circles were afforded primary status throughout the URI network; innovation was welcomed and encouraged; ambitious fundraising was embraced for the first time; and the prevailing spirit throughout the URI family began to resemble the prevailing spirit of adventure that marked URI's founding experience. So I felt at home again. Now I am genuinely enthusiastic about what lies ahead for URI and can't wait to be part of the new day.

Chapter 22
Don't Go There

When I was in seminary studying to become a priest, I asked one of my professors about people of other religions, "Would they be saved?" Rather than answering the question, he simply said, "Don't go there. If you start thinking about people of other religions, you will probably end up in some vague kind of universalism that believes everyone will be saved—a kind of syncretism whereby all of the beliefs of all of the faiths are thrown into a Cuisinart and blended into a soupy theological mess without substance!" Since the intent behind my question was only casual and inquisitive, I stopped thinking about it for thirty-five years. But by then, I was dealing with people of other faiths on a regular basis, and the question came up with more urgency for me. My professor had warned, "Don't go there!" But I went there.

What was the fear that lurked behind my professor's warning? I have concluded over time that the fear was not that I might come to assume that people of other faiths could be saved by God for eternal life. The great fear was that my own basic core belief would be eroded, gradually, if I associated with people of other faiths. My professor worried that I might lose my soul. To be the best Christian that I could possibly be, I would need to be indoctrinated in its faith, sing its songs, hear its Scriptures, and be nurtured by its community. Were I to take myself out of this context, perhaps I would lose the essence of my baptism into the Body of Christ. I could lose my birthright as a Christian.

Has that actually happened? I made a vow as an ordained deacon. I made a vow as a priest. I made a vow as a bishop. Now that I live daily in a community of people of all of the faiths, have my vows lessened or vanished from my resolve? Has my faith evaporated? I would have to examine all of this, one vow at a time.

On St. Barnabas Day, June 11, 1961, at St. John's Episcopal Church, Huntington, West Virginia I stood before the Bishop of West Virginia and made my vows as a deacon. A deacon's task is always, "to serve all people, particularly the poor, the weak, the sick and the lonely." To serve! That was my primitive prayer as a boy growing up in Huntington. Together with the members of our parish, each Sunday I would say these words. "…giving up ourselves to Thy service." From the beginning, I understood that my vocation was to be of service to God. I had to be ready to give up something of myself in order to go about that service. Intuitively, very diaconal! My career might be as a priest, or a bishop, or an interfaith founder. But my vocation was to be of service to God.

Thousands of house calls and hospital calls later, after feeding tens of thousands of hungry people and housing 1,500 homeless a night for decades, I had abundant opportunities to fulfill this diaconal vow. But what about entering the interfaith domain? Would I become an inter-religious bureaucrat far removed from "the poor, the weak, the sick and the lonely?" To my delight I have found that our URI Cooperation Circles accomplish very practical deeds of servant-hood, like caring for orphans off the streets, responding to disasters, caring for victims of AIDS and cholera, fighting for the rights of the indigenous, advocating for abused women, and hundreds of more actions that are deeply humanitarian. My journey of servant-hood that started from the Christian faith and grew to include the life of interfaith, has been seamless. Nothing was left behind. It all became part of the same. My diaconate has stayed intact.

When I was a boy going to church camp in the summers just after World War II, I encountered the most noble, inspiring group of adults whom I had ever met. They were all parish priests: fun, spiritual, intellectually inquisitive, and concerned for people. Griffin Callahan, Craig Eder, Frank Rowley, Fred Valentine are all gone now, but back then, they captured my imagination. Not only did I look up to them, but also I wanted to be a parish priest just like they were. So I went off to seminary to follow in their footsteps.

On St. Thomas Day, December 21, 1961, at St. Matthew's Episcopal Church in Wheeling, West Virginia, I stood in front of the Bishop of West Virginia and made my vow to be a priest. In the examination of a priest, these words are said, "As a priest…. You are to love and serve the people among whom you work…." At the time, I assumed that those words must have meant that I was supposed to love and serve the people of a parish where I was working. So much energy is required to love and serve Episcopalians! It didn't dawn on me that I might be called to love and serve people of other religions, cultures and races. So, no matter where I went or where I focused my attention, all roads would lead back to parish priesthood, specifically the parish where I was assigned.

When I was a chaplain at a tuberculosis hospital in Columbus, Ohio in the Clinical Pastoral Education program, I was involved, as were all of the other chaplains, in intensive counseling, questioning, and group dynamics. At the end of the program all of us were given an opportunity to sign up for advance work so that we might become trainers in clinical pastoral training. Some of the chaplains signed on, and found their niche in a hospital. I had learned a lot, but I wanted to take my insights and get back to parish ministry.

When the Black Civil Rights Movement came along, as well as the controversies over the Vietnam War, I got involved and learned a lot. As the head of the ministerial association in Weirton, W. Va., it fell to me to lead the campaign for open housing. Formerly, blacks could live only next to the steel mills, but we made it possible for everyone to find housing in cleaner areas. As for the Vietnam War, I struggled with a deeply divided and vocal congregation in Washington, D.C. Some of my priest friends got so caught up in the pursuit of social justice issues that they abandoned the parish priesthood and spent the rest of their lives marching and advocating. As for me, I went back to parish priesthood.

With the advent of sensitivity training, organizational development, and the small group skills movement, I signed on and benefited greatly. But as this training morphed into the human potential movement of the 1960s and '70s, several of my clergy colleagues who were deeply attracted to it left their parishes and were seldom seen again in the Church. This training was tremendously helpful to me as I continued on in parish priesthood.

But what about interfaith work? Is it a temporary offset? Does it have any redeeming feature for a Christian parish? Should I take what is translatable and helpful and then head back home? Or is it possible to have a Christian ministry and an interfaith ministry at the same time? One little thought: one of the priest's jobs in the twenty-first century is to help parishioners live in an interfaith world. Schools, workplaces, neighborhoods, entertainments, sports teams, jails, and hospitals are almost all going to be interfaith. No longer can priests only help parishioners live in an Episcopal ethos (or in any of the other exclusive religious cultures).

So today, as a retired bishop, I sit in our parish church each Sunday with my wife, Mary, and I search the Scriptures and the hymns to discover what are the latent interfaith themes that hide just below the surface, themes that in a few years will be celebrated. Oh yes, the interfaith themes are there. Usually they abide in the use of the word, "all." That word appears over 800 times in the Bible. Negatively, as in "all have sinned and come short of the glory of God" (Romans 3:23), and positively, as in "…so that God may be all in all" (I Corinthians 15:28). Occasionally, I celebrate the sacraments and preach, but usually my parish priesthood sits within me in an interfaith office in San Francisco and tries to figure out how to reconcile my faith with all of the different faiths. That seems priestly enough for an old man.

On St. Michael and All Angels Day, September 29, 1979, at Grace Cathedral in San Francisco, I was consecrated a bishop in the Church of God. Hands were laid on my head, mostly by bishops of the western United States and several others from the east coast. My vow? "A bishop...is called to be one with the apostles in proclaiming Christ's resurrection…to testify to Christ's sovereignty as Lord of lords and King of kings." I could certainly do that in church from the pulpit or from the altar. But what about out in the interfaith world? How to proclaim Christ's resurrection in an ashram? How to testify to Christ's sovereignty with the Dalai Lama in Dharamsala or with Muslims in the Jami Mosque in New Delhi? What words to use, words that would be understood? How to translate the essence of these words without having triumphant human arrogance get in the way and create an enduring hostility? How to be true to the deepest instincts of the Christian faith and not "give away the store"? These are hard questions for a bishop who would one day step into the interfaith arena!

I did believe and still do believe that the perfect Christ is Lord of lords and King of kings. Why? Because the perfect Christ is One with the Creator of all; is the Beginning and the End! But, the perfect Christ is known imperfectly by limited people with our misleading languages and partial thoughts, expressed in segments of moving time. On the one hand I believe that at the throne of God there will be nothing that contradicts the perfect Christ. One the other hand I believe that among the myriad aspects of the perfect Christ, the highest and best for all of us are the attributes of love and generosity. For me, those two aspects have no limits. In the end, I believe that no one will live far from the love of God and the generosity of God, as portrayed in the perfect Christ's death and resurrection.

Doing the job of a bishop is partly a matter of just arriving at the right time and place. I had to drive myself to eighty-six congregations, forty schools, thirty social ministries, across six bridges, and into six counties for twenty-seven years. The folks in the pews were not so much concerned about my orthodoxy as they were about whether or not I would show up. In twenty-seven years, I never missed a Sunday and only had four sick days, so the folks gave me a good grade on attendance.

On the other hand, a bishop is the agent of unity for all of the constituents—liberal, conservative, far out, scholarly, activists, foreign born of many nations, gay, straight, charismatic, high church, low church, angry, and friendly. So when their bishop begins to head in an interfaith direction, some people worry about him or her becoming a false shepherd and leading the folks astray.

When my role as a bishop took an interfaith turn, all kinds of alarm buttons went off for lots of people. A couple of people wrote books accusing me of being a megalomaniac. And a radio talk show host in San Antonio, Texas, introduced me to his audience with these words: "You all know how the United Nations wants to take over all nations. Well here is a bishop from San Francisco—and you all know what kind of people live in San Francisco, ha, ha—he wants to take over all of the religions and make himself the head of the United Religions. Ladies and gentlemen, here is Bishop William Swing." Sixty minutes of fury followed. At the end I asked the host a question, "If you ever found out the truth about the United Religions Initiative, would you have the courage to tell your audience the truth?" The host went so ballistic that the owner of the radio station called me the next day to apologize and to offer to give me an hour to tell the audience about the URI.

I once gave a talk at the University of Wisconsin, Whitewater Campus and afterwards I had to run across a parking lot hurriedly to catch a plane for another talk. A young man who had been in the audience began to run beside me and said, "Bishop Swing, my father is an Episcopal priest, and he thinks that you are the anti-Christ. But I don't think you are the anti-Christ. I think you're nuts!" (I made my flight.)

Nevertheless, I was appreciated by a presiding bishop (equivalent to "Archbishop") of the Episcopal Church of the United States of America. In 1996 he invited me for dinner, just the two of us, to tell me that he had traveled across the country prior to his forthcoming retirement, asking people who should be the next presiding bishop. He said that my name came up most often. So he wanted to know if I was interested in the job of presiding over the Episcopal Church. It took a split send for me to say "no." I told him, "I could think of ten bishops who could do a good job as Presiding Bishop, but I couldn't think of one other person in the world who was trying to create a United Religions.

I have a recurring nightmare about a battlefield after "the big fight." The fog is lifting just enough at daybreak so that I can see that the Shia have annihilated the Sunni, or vice versa. The Christians have annihilated the Jews, or vice versa. The Catholics have annihilated the Protestants, or vice versa. The Buddhists have annihilated the Muslims, or vice versa. The Hindus have annihilated the Sikhs, or vice versa. Perhaps they've done it with a nuclear weapon, or conversion campaign, or a crusade, or an effort to obtain religious purity! After everyone has been killed in the Name of God, God walks onto the battlefield. Why? To thank them for their devotion? No; to cry. And to lament that while there was still such a thing as life, they chose not to discover their kinship, but rather to surrender to their death wish, in God's Name. Judgment, in my dream, follows the cry of God. Did we chose kinship or did we choose death wish? God will decide.

Over the years people have come to me saying, "Okay, bishop, what do you think of this? Jesus said, 'I am the Way, the Truth and the Life. No one comes to the Father but by me.' (John 14:6) No one, not your Jewish or your Muslim buddies." I always answer by saying that it depended on the sound of his voice, when he said it. Was his voice saying, "You can't go to heaven unless you belong to my club?" Or was his voice saying, "You can't get from where you are to the throne of God unless you go through law-keeping, justice, mercy, sacrifice, and compassion. That is the only way to the throne of God, and I am that Way." By his voice, was he creating an exclusive club or a path open to everyone?

I always hear two different voices coming from Jesus. One voice summons his full authority. "He rebuked the man with an unclean spirit and ordered the unclean spirits to come out of him, and the man convulsed and cried with a loud voice." (Mark 1:26) To Lazarus in the tomb, he shouted, "Come out!" (John 11:43) To the child of a religious leader, a child that had been pronounced dead, he commanded her saying, "Little girl, I say to you, arise." (Mark 5:41) To the trembling Thomas he said, "Put your finger here and see my hands. Reach out your hand and put it in my side. Do not doubt but believe." (John 20:25) My faith as a Christian has been fashioned by the force of Jesus' voice.

On the other hand, my interfaith work has been inspired by the other voice of Jesus, the voice of "echoes of mercy, whispers of love" (from the hymn, *Blessed Assurance*). When he said, "Love your enemies" (Luke 6:26); "...Blessed are the poor, are the merciful, are those who hunger and thirst after righteousness, are those who mourn" (Matthew: Chapter 5); "...Do you begrudge me my generosity?" (Matthew 20:15); "...And he took the little children into his arms and blessed them" (Mark 10:16); "...Inasmuch as you have done it unto the least of these my brethren, you have done it unto me" (Matthew 25:40). Jesus had a quiet voice of total embrace that propels me into a much larger world than only the Christian community.

The central question then confronts me on my quest. If I venture out into no man's land, out there on the battlefield where religious violence has prevailed for centuries, will I meet some people from the other side who have also heard echoes of mercy and whispers of love from their most esteemed Divine Voice? Interfaith isn't a lack of faith; it is a leap of faith. The Psalmist in 42:7 writes that "Deep calls to deep." Will the depths of me find common humanity in the depths of my religious foe? The purest interfaith question is whether or not we have the courage to jump out of our well-dug trenches and expect to find kindred spirits from the enemy lines rushing toward the barbed wire ready to embrace us?

The interfaith challenge is to grow a heart for the assumed Oneness that exists in atoms and Muslims, galaxies and Buddhists, nature and Jews, universes and Universalists. Is there, after all, a vast Oneness that exists in the mind of God and beats in the original heart, and inflates and holds all things together in the gravity of love? I believe in an ultimate community that flourishes within and beyond all communities, a community that responds to echoes of mercy and whispers of love.

As things turned out, the URI has developed no stake in doctrine, or dogma, or belief systems, or history of religious grievances. Its sole function has been to get people of differing faiths together, every day, all over the world, in order to address local concerns and/or global good. Its focus was to be on increasing the health of civil society. URI is about civilization, not salvation. If we waited around for religions to solve their problems before taking common action, we would wait forever. URI was created to give people immediate opportunity to work together across religious lines.

As a bishop considering the long trajectory of time, I do worry about interfaith becoming a watered-down substitute for religion. It would thus become just one more competing religion, rather than offering the world a means of cooperation among existing religions. The rise of interfaith seminaries, and interfaith congregations, and interfaith music, implies to me that another religion is being created out of all of the religions, perhaps an easy religion of little gravitas. In the candy store of interfaith possibilities, I can imagine some hungry person walking in and ordering ten cents worth of Buddhism, fifteen cents worth of Catholicism, a nickel worth of ethical humanism, a quarter worth of Quakerism, and on and on. Cutting off all of the flowers of religion in order to make a bouquet that lasts for a few days is sadly different from allowing the flowers to stay rooted and then to create a garden. But all of that will evolve as it wills.

And who am I to sound an alarm? My professor warned me, "Don't go there." And I went.

Chapter 23
The Unfinished URI

Former Israeli President Shimon Peres visited Pope Francis I in the Vatican on September 4, 2014. According to the Catholic News Service, Peres called for the creation of a United Religions to counter religious extremism throughout the world. "What we need," said Peres, "is an organization of United Religions to counteract these terrorists who kill in the name of their faith. In the past, most wars were motivated by the idea of nationhood. Today, however, wars are incited above all using religion as an excuse."

Who knows? Someday in the future, there just might be a mounting call for a United Religions.

Nowadays, when I look at the original concept of a United Religions, in my mind (and truly, it is only in my mind) I see it not so much an organization but as a society, a multinational society of principled faith and interfaith communities which aims to enrich local communities and civil society. Thus, it is a society within and across societies. United Religions isn't a building or bureaucracy, a brand or a business. United Religions is a worldwide society of people of various faith traditions who yearn to heal religious divides and make life healthier at local levels and global levels. United Religions doesn't exist, but it is incubating in the URI.

Thomas Jefferson, James Madison and other early American leaders looked into the mirror of history at all of the religious wars and resulting carnage and asked themselves how they could build a society that would fundamentally reduce the prospects for religiously-motivated violence. Their answer was stated in two principles: religious freedom for everyone, and no religion will ever be the established religion of this nation.

Someday, religious leaders will ask themselves a similar kind of question. How can we assist a society in fundamentally reducing the prospects of religiously-motivated violence? Religions can't ask that question yet because some are holding out to be the established religion in one country or another, or to dethrone an established religion, or to deprive other religions of freedom. But someday, religious leaders will understand what the statesmen of this nation understood, namely that ordinary life is degraded because religion can't tolerate religions. Someday, the people of the world will rise up and demand a fundamental change because the insanity of religiously-motivated violence only brings disaster.

A United Religions Initiative requires the faithful of the grassroots. A United Religions requires religious leaders. If the religious leaders don't step up, then the grassroots need to begin the transformation from violence to cooperation. A URI is the first big step toward a UR.

Meanwhile, within the nations that feel the effects of perpetual religious violence there is still a desperate need for a multinational society of principled interfaith communities that yearn to heal religious divisions and make life healthier at local and global levels. They will not bring about a religious version of the United Nations, nor a big bureaucracy in San Francisco. The United Religions Initiative is a stopgap measure of hope and action until the time when it dawns on religious leaders that what is needed is religious freedom, and no religion ever being the established religion of a country. URI is the best option in our present predicament. A United Religions, a multinational society of religious freedom and guardians against established religion, should be the ultimate goal, in my opinion.

What fascinates me now about URI is how we figure out a creative organizational solution that honors our DNA of spontaneity, and at the same time encourages the professional disciplines needed to achieve the greatest expansion of our work. How do we keep the Hub and Global Staff at a minimum size and at the same time, farm out the role of centralizing to Multiple Cooperation Circles or to "Resource Cooperation Circles"? I am sure that we can succeed in this discovery. We have gone from a Host Committee, to an Interim Global Council, to a Global Council—and along the way, created Regional Structures and a President's Council, and a Joint Steering Committee. Always evolving! We will experiment until we get this right. It will be fun for me to participate.

As I approach the end of my URI career, I think about all of the people of URI whose genius and energy created something desperately needed all over the world. I cherish these friends and colleagues. Together, we have done and are doing and, God-willing, will keep on doing something good. I hope that it pleases and honors God. As for what I started out to accomplish—namely, a United Religions—I realize that I have to take an incomplete in this course. Yet, in my daydreams I can vaguely see the ingredients of a United Religions and the outline of some sort of magnetic field of the sacred that will draw us together. But I can't connect the dots just now. Perhaps through some revelatory inspiration, or because of a horrific global disaster, the people of faiths will at last discover each other and live together more charitably.

As for me, the bookends are February nights. One was a restless night in San Francisco in February 1993 that changed my life. The other was a night of sleep in February 2014 when Shias and Sunnis in Baghdad formed a Cooperation Circle! As the 1940s song says, "I'll buy that dream!"

At the beginning of this quest, I had three challenges: to announce the vision, to find the people who could bring it to reality, and to pay for it. All of that happened. Now what, in 2014? URI is in its fourteenth year, and I am in my seventy-eighth year. What is there now about URI that makes me bounce out of bed each morning eager to get to work? It is the unfinished part. I am absolutely fascinated about the big issues that we have kicked down the road figuring to solve at a later time. Today is later time for me. Here are the big three unfinished issues:

1. Funding URI in the future
2. Finding the voice of URI in the future
3. Figuring out the best organizational design for URI in the future

1. Funding URI in the future

It takes a certain amount of money, approximately four million dollars a year, to hold this large global network together at a minimum level. In theory, URI is a grassroots organization and so this money should come from the grass roots. But no monies come from this source. In theory, URI should have an endowment of $90 million to assure this minimum financial level. But the endowment is presently about $300,000. In theory, URI assists community building among religions, so religions might think about picking up a share of the URI costs. But URI has an unwritten policy not to accept money from religions. If we received from one and not another, it would be awfully hard for us to create a level playing field among the religions. To add to the difficulty, URI hasn't had a regular committee that strategizes about fundraising. We haven't had a Global Assembly in six years, and none is planned anytime soon because we don't know how to pay for it. Up to now, URI has lived year to year simply trying to pay all of the bills. Amazingly, all bills have been paid and there is no debt. Where did this money come from? Answer: mostly from the people whom I approached.

I had a long running head start in relationship to money. When I was five years old and our family lived in one room, inside the clubhouse of Spring Valley Country Club in Huntington, West Virginia I would go outside early in the morning, or in the late afternoon, to play in a tiny creek at the bottom of a hill. Golfers had to hit balls over that creek, and when they failed, their wayward golf balls hid in the tall grass or in the muddy water. Also, crawdads and frogs lived there as well. So, when everyone had departed the golf course, I would go searching for treasures of squirmy creatures and abandoned balls. Usually I brought home a generous harvest. It was a great feeling, and it took root in my unconscious because it kept showing up in my dreams over the years.

In my recurring dream, the setting was always the tiny creek at the bottom of the hill. What happened in my dreams was that every time I turned over a rock or searched through the weeds, I would always find money in the form of coins, coins of all denominations. I never counted the money but I was certain that it amounted to a lot. It always left me with a great feeling. I had no idea what the dream meant but the impression it left was clear. I was going to have a grand time collecting money.

In reality, I never made much money. As a matter of fact, I always settled for a minimum salary wherever I worked, which led to some heated domestic conversations. Some for instances: As an Assistant, I made $3,000 a year plus housing. As a Vicar of a small congregation, I started out making $5,000 a year plus housing. As a Rector of a large parish, I started out making $7,500 a year and lived in the church's house ("the Rectory"). As Bishop of the Diocese of California my starting salary in 1980 was $45,000 a year plus housing. In URI, I worked for no salary or benefits for thirteen years.

Why? Because I figured that if I focused on keeping my vows to God, God would make sure that my family wouldn't starve. This has been a private fact up to now.

In reality, I have spent my adult life up to my neck in raising money and lots of it. It was always money for good causes, such as an intensive care unit, a homeless center, housing for immigrants, a capital development bank, and more. At the end of my tenure as the seventh bishop of California, I figured that about a billion dollars had come into and circulated through the Diocese, and a goodly portion of that money was directly or indirectly tied to my consistency in keeping my vows. My personal motto was always the words of St. Paul, who said, "…as having nothing and making many rich." (2 Corinthians 6:10.) My overriding thought was that if I lived by faith, it would allow others to have faith in me and my leadership. And if that was the case we could build almost anything together.

Now we are entering a stage of life for URI when it has to go far beyond my fundraising efforts. The signs of this are just now appearing on the horizon. One member of the President's Council, without being asked, made a pledge of a million dollars a year for five years. Another member of the President's Council similarly pledged five million dollars over five years, but paid it all at once at the beginning. At the same time, various people are writing URI into their wills because they see that URI will be in business for the long haul. They feel emboldened to invest in our future. And critical to a new day for URI and money, URI's second Executive Director, the Rev. Victor Kazanjian, Jr. has just arrived and is getting a team of people together to develop a strategy for fundraising, and he is excited about making asks himself. Finally, we have established a way for individuals to contribute as members of URI and to make smaller donations on a regular basis. So the stage is being set for three sources of funds to cover URI's steady expansion: major gifts, endowment gifts, and a large number of smaller gifts from members.

Does the lack of money hold URI back? Absolutely! One of the things that fuels our growth and effectiveness is getting the whole family together at a Global Assembly, as we did in Rio de Janeiro, Brazil in 2003 and in Mayapur, India in 2008. Smaller Regional Assemblies do a good job of this each year, but nothing takes the place of seeing the whole family at once and catching the excitement of a Global Assembly. Also, we have had so much growth in the size of our regions that we are now required to create subregions to administer the burgeoning work. But we don't have the money to fund the offices of many of the subregions. The only thing holding us back is money. So the bottom line is that URI has gone as far as it can go by trusting in my fundraising prowess alone. Now is the time for an expanded approach. Just as the time came for the URI vision and work to go beyond me, even so now the time has come for the task of raising money to be picked up by a far great number of people.

A priest friend of mine from Keyser, West Virginia, told me about how he would go down to the railroad station every afternoon at 3:45 and just sit in the parking lot. At 4:00 p.m., he left. Finally someone asked him, "Why do you sit in the parking lot every afternoon at 3:45 at the train station?" The answer was: "Every day the C and O Train comes through Keyser at 3:50 p.m. and it is the only thing that moves in this town that I don't have to push." Somehow that story resonates for me.

2. Finding the Voice of URI in the Future

A young Muslim man stood up in a meeting of the Global Staff and Global Council in Amman, Jordon in 2010, and with pulsating emotion he exclaimed, "How can this group that cares so deeply about religious freedom meet in the Middle East in the midst of all of the religious and other injustices exercised against Muslims here, and you will not say a word?" Of course the Jewish Israelis quickly made their point about suicide bombers and their unwillingness to recognize Israel. And the entire gathering launched into a heated discussion about what kind of official statement we could make. Actually, we did come up with something, but it was bland and satisfied no one. That brought up the ever-challenging question of how URI can find an appropriate voice with which to speak to the world.

As we had done in similar instances before, we gave this question to a committee of people from around the world, a committee made up of people who had emphatic opinions on the subject. Their task was to think through all of the dimensions, and try to figure out how we could arrive at a common voice on deeply significant, divisive matters. And like the committees before them which had been so commissioned, they never met and gave up on the task without a whimper.

Lots of issues here! URI is not basically an advocacy organization, so why bother with ever making a statement? Our job, usually, is to originate local action, carried out by local people. What difference would it make if URI did make a statement? Who would care? And who could legitimately speak on behalf of everyone in URI? Could the Global Council? The Executive Director? The Founder and President? Are we a centralized or a diffuse organization? In our bylaws, no one was given that responsibility. The reason for this is that when we were writing the Charter, we couldn't come to a conclusion.

Would URI statements tend to come from a progressive or a conservative bias? The World Council of Churches has often been described as espousing a liberal tone. On the other hand, when historic religions get together they can be conservative in the extreme. On this latter point, I remember one time being in Rome listening to discussion between the Roman Catholics in the West and the Orthodox in the East, debating about the date of Easter. It usually falls on different Sundays for each group because they each use different calendars. One side offered to change their own calendar and have Easter on the same day as the other church, saying that it would give the world a symbol of unity. But the leaders of the other group said, "Absolutely not! If we celebrated Easter on the same day as you, it would give the world a symbol of unity. But since we are not in unity with you, we need to give the world a symbol of disunity." I wondered to myself how long this discussion has been going on. And the answer is, about a thousand years.

URI already speaks in general in its Purpose Statement about "ending religious violence." So it would be fitting to make statements of general moral value. The problem comes when the statement clearly implies the guilt of one party and the innocence of another.

From time to time, the Global Council will make a general statement to the public, and so will the Executive Director and myself, as the President. But these tend to be generalities.

In contrast to the overall constraints, there are no restraints on Cooperation Circles. They can make any statement they want, even if it is contradicted by other Cooperation Circles. We say that the greatest amount of authority is located in the smallest unit—namely, in a Cooperation Circle—and their voices are independent and authorized. For instance, on June 2, 2011 one of our Cooperation Circles in the U.S. issued a call to action about hydraulic fracturing saying: "We call upon governmental bodies to place moratoriums on the use of hydraulic fracturing until it is better understood, and until technological safeguards and proper regulatory controls and oversight are in place…. We also call upon the government bodies to hold the companies accountable for any liability to individuals and water systems that are polluted through this process."

In 2011, the Cooperation Circle entitled Voices for a World Free of Nuclear Weapons issued *A Call of Conscience*. The written statement reads: "We believe that the indiscriminate, destructive effects of nuclear weapons render them incompatible with civilized values and international law. The threat to use them to annihilate vast numbers of innocent people and inflict indescribable suffering and environmental destruction is immoral and contrary to the purposes for which the blessings of life have been given to us. Our goal is to achieve the universal, legally enforceable, nondiscriminatory, and verifiable elimination of nuclear weapons."

A distinct possibility of a URI voice exists in the area of local interfaith organizations in the U.S. coming together under the umbrella of URI to express a united point of advocacy and information sharing. Almost every city of medium-to-large size in the United States has a citywide interfaith organization. In my earlier travels, I would invite such local interfaith organizations to become Cooperation Circles of URI. Almost one hundred percent of them refused, saying that they considered URI to be a competitor. With so much rejection, I set that idea aside. Over a decade later, the situation has reversed itself, not because of URI's persistence in inviting local interfaith organizations, but because local interfaith organizations want to have a global dimension. Now hardly a month goes by without some citywide interfaith organization applying to become a URI Cooperation Circle. URI doesn't charge dues and doesn't insist on one approach! Instead, it offers access to a world of local interfaith organizations where each can learn from the other. URI acts as an Internet for them. Someday, when this universe of local interfaith organizations ripens, the potential exists to create a powerful interfaith voice. That might seem a long way off, but in my experience, that day might happen soon.

It is only a matter of time before statements that will be interpreted as being the voice of URI will be caught up in a swirl of controversy. At such a time, we will have to spell out for ourselves and for the world where URI is on the matter of having a voice. With a fourteen-to-eighteen percent growth rate in each of the first fourteen years of URI's life, someday the URI umbrella will be so large that various forces will lobby URI to make statements that would enhance such lobbies. In the meantime, there is growing urgency to find our voice—a clear and disciplined voice! I am greatly looking forward to being part of this discussion, and seeing where we end up.

3. Figuring Out the Best Organizational Design for the Future of URI

I smile when I think about the first layer of organizing in URI. It was called "Host Committee" and was informal to a fault. The members were anyone who showed up for the meetings, which took place every couple of weeks. Y'all come! A young Korean Buddhist appeared—Jin Wol Lee, who was studying for a doctorate in Berkeley. Later on, he would become URI's Regional Coordinator in South Korea. An old man from Salt Lake City, Utah, would ride the bus for two days to make these meetings. When this amazingly diverse group gathered, we launched into discussions about the destiny that lay ahead and we tried to make strategic decisions. At one time we looked into what name our organization should be called—should it be United Religions or United Religions Organization or United Religions Initiative? We decided to lay claim to the name United Religions, with the understanding that we would call ourselves the United Religions Initiative only for a short time, time enough to write a Charter and actually become the United Religions. Of course, some enterprising person discovered our plan and hurriedly incorporated the name "United Religions." So it cost us $10,000 to buy it from him.

The Host Committee was freewheeling, fluid, and flexible, and it established the genetic code of what was to follow. Its purpose was to be of total service to that which was about to be born. The amateur flair of this group assumed that someday it would have to bow out and that a far more professional organization would take its place. At its roots, the United Religions Initiative would be an organization always moving from high spontaneity to more rigorous discipline.

Dee Hock was the perfect fit for the development of our Charter Writing, since he specialized in Chaos and Order, or Chaordic Alliance. He worked to keep the tension between the two. He used to say to me, "Someday when this thing is built, you will go to sleep one night and the next morning you will wake up and the URI will have grown. It has to be built on the dynamic of nature which struggles in multiple dimensions to assure life for itself."

Dee was right. One week in February 2014, I went to sleep one night and the next morning I discovered that URI had six more Cooperation Circles. One in Baghdad, Iraq where our folks are getting Sunni and Shia religious leaders together! One in Kasserine, Tunisia, the country where the Arab Spring started in 2010! And one in Silicon Valley!

The tough challenge comes from building in more professional competence without squashing the soul of the spontaneous community. Without thinking about it, the arteries can begin to harden. For instance, The Hub in San Francisco looks out and sees women's issues being addressed in Cooperation Circles all over the world. One instinct is to say, let's create a Department of Women's Issues to coordinate everyone; or, let's create a Department of Youth Leaders; or, a Department of the Environment; or, a Department of Indigenous Work—and on and on. Soon there would be a growing bureaucracy that would require more command and control by the Hub. Then all of a sudden the spirit that gave birth to URI would have morphed into a typical bureaucratic organization. And order would triumph over chaos.

Epilogue
Whatever Happened To The Dreamer?

Upon my retirement as Bishop of the Diocese of California eight years ago, Mary and I moved eight blocks from the golf course where I am a member. Often in the afternoon I can be found on the first tee, joined by Ambassador Michael Armacost. He bets the endowment of his college, Carleton College, and I wager the endowment of my college, Kenyon College, and we trash talk and discuss the world scene for seven holes. Why seven? Because we are too lazy to hike the hills on two of the holes! Whoever wins sings the fight song of his alma mater as we walk off the last green. As yet, no college has ever benefitted.

Sometimes in the "big gang" of golfers on Saturday mornings I have shot my age, a much heralded achievement in the world of golf. Say that I am seventy-eight years old and shoot a seventy-eight—well, in golf that is admirable. But most times I shoot a score that is much closer to my IQ.

A friend and I won a prestigious local tournament—three times. When I went into the pro shop I told the pro that we needed to lose next year because I only have four friends left at the club. To which the pro replied, "Name them."

Nowadays, if King Abdullah bin Abdul Aziz of Saudi Arabia invites me to take part in the dedication of his Intercultural, Interreligious Centre in Vienna, I go. If I am invited to participate in the dedication of the Museum of the History of Polish Jews in Warsaw, I go. If I am offered an opportunity to speak around the world, I go.

As for the Episcopal Diocese of California, the custom is that former bishops stay out of the way. This works well. Mary and I are very regular parishioners at St. Paul's Episcopal Church, Burlingame, California and we love that worshipping community. Since Mary has been very ill most of the past two years, I celebrate the Sacrament at her bedside quite often. She refers to me as her Resident Priest. Occasionally, I will officiate at a funeral, or a baptism, or a marriage. From time to time I will be invited around the country to preach. But none of that very often! My ordination vows have taken root in my innermost parts and I figure that I keep all my vows current through bringing the mark of a Christian to interfaith situations.

We have three grandchildren who live in the area, so they bring great richness into our lives. And I am able to work manually in the rich soil of our backyard.

When I was in Seminary, we had a professor who would refer to a gravestone in England that said, "He was born a man and died as a greengrocer." The professor would stare at us with great conviction and say, "Never let this be said of you. Don't lose your humanity in the pursuit of the sacred. You were born a man, be a man, and die a man, not a priest." Obviously, his statement has stayed with me for a lifetime.

As for the end of life, I don't think that God paints by the numbers. Judgment and mercy are in the ultimate hands of the Artist Of Life whose pallette abounds in graceful and riveting dark hues of beauty. We are, all of us together, in some ways, God's masterpieces, detailed across a wide canvas, responding at each brush stroke of life and decision-making. The story is told of an Archbishop of Canterbury who was walking down the street and was confronted by a drunk who asked, "Buddy, are you saved?" The Archbishop referred to one Greek word for salvation and said, "If you mean that word, then when Jesus died on the cross for my salvation, yes, I am saved." Then he referred to another Greek word for salvation and said, "If you mean that word, then when I was incorporated by baptism into Jesus's death and resurrection, then yes I am saved." Then he referred to a third Greek word for salvation, and he said, "If you mean that word, it has to do with the final Day of Judgment when the secrets of all hearts will be revealed, then no, I haven't any idea if I will be saved." That Archbishop speaks for me.

And when I look around at my Muslim, Atheist, Jewish, Indigenous, and Hindu friends, and I wonder where they will be headed in their final hours, I collapse before a Mystery that is far beyond my pitifully limited perspective. I am content to respond as best I can to the story of God that I have been told, the story that comes close to being what my highest imaginings of God to be. Then my marching orders are to make this place on earth as close to heaven as I can dream, and as I have been taught. In this latter task they are all my colleagues, the people of all the faiths.

As for URI, I walk around with a feeling that is deeper than pride or humility. It is something like holding a newborn baby in your arms and feeling, oh my, it's alive! Isn't it beautiful! What a privilege to be standing here at this precious moment. Generation to generation! I am in awe.

Mary and the Bishop with Secretary George Schultz and Charlotte Schultz, above; below, with Dr. Hans Kung

With Pope John Paul II in Rome

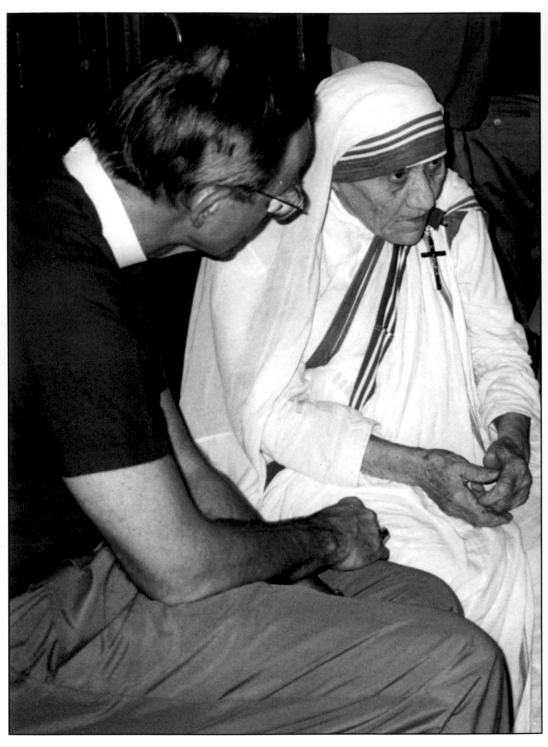

With Mother Theresa in Calcutta

With His Holiness The Dalai Lama in Dharmasala

With The Shankaracharya of Kanchipuram

With His Holiness Shenouda III, the Coptic Pope, in Cairo

Dee Hock, above; below, the One Day Conference in Pakistan

In Geneva, above; below, Mary in Istanbul with Easter eggs

At the Maramon Convention in India, above; below, with Charles Gibbs and T.D. Singh in India

As Christmas was
approaching in 2007 we
were enjoying the tango in
Buenos Aires
when an unexpected
invitation arrived. The
local cardinal wanted us to
bring our interfaith
friends to his cathedral for
a prayer service.

And we did.

The Swings' 2013 Christmas Card, front and back panels

Left to right: Bishop William E. Swing, Swami Pareshananda, Raul Mamani,
Sheik Beytullah Cholak, Rabbi Arieh Sztokman and Cardinal Jorge Mario Bergoglio

The Cardinal was Jorge Mario Bergoglio.

But at this Christmas he is well known as Pope Francis I.

What a divine surprise!

Come to think of it, that is what Christmas is all about:

A Divine Surprise!

With love from the dancing Swings

Christmas 2013

The Swings' 2013 Christmas Card, inside panels

The friendly study of all religions is the sacred duty of every individual.

— Mahatma Gandhi

With Iftekhar Hai, lecturing on Mecca

Mary in New Delhi, above; below, at a Sikh temple in New Delhi

The Oxford talk with Dr. Marcus Braybooke, above; below, the Stanford gathering of 1997

The Stanford gathering of 1998, above; below, the 1999 gathering

At the Stanford gathering, above; below, His Holiness The Dalai Lama with Mary

Appendix

Charter of United Religions Initiative
        Preamble, Purpose and Principles
        Organizational Design

Commentary on Preamble, Purpose and Principles

Evolution of URI Organizational Design

History of Proposals for a United Religions 1893-1996

Tribute to Charles Gibbs

Peace Comes Piecemeal

President's Council Prayer

Preamble

We, people of diverse religions, spiritual expressions and indigenous traditions throughout the world, hereby establish the United Religions Initiative to promote enduring, daily, interfaith cooperation, to end religiously motivated violence and to create cultures of peace,justice and healing for the Earth and all living beings.

We respect the uniqueness of each tradition, and differences of practice or belief.

We value voices that respect others, and believe that sharing our values and wisdom can lead us to act for the good of all.

We believe that our religious, spiritual lives, rather than dividing us, guide us to build community and respect for one another.

Therefore, as interdependent people rooted in our traditions, we now unite for the benefit of our Earth community.

We unite to build cultures of peace and justice.

We unite to heal and protect the Earth.

We unite to build safe places for conflict resolution, healing and reconciliation.

We unite to support freedom of religion and spiritual expression, and the rights of all individuals and peoples as set forth in international law.

We unite in responsible cooperative action to bring the

wisdom and values of our religions, spiritual expressions and indigenous traditions to bear on the economic, environmental, political and social challenges facing our Earth community.

We unite to provide a global opportunity for participation by all people, especially by those whose voices are not often heard.

We unite to celebrate the joy of blessings and the light of wisdom in both movement and stillness.

We unite to use our combined resources only for nonviolent, compassionate action, to awaken to our deepest truths, and to manifest love and justice among all life in our Earth community.

Purpose

The purpose of the United Religions Initiative is to promote enduring, daily, interfaith cooperation; to end religiously motivated violence; and to create cultures of peace, justice, and healing for the Earth, and all living beings.

Principles

1. The URI is a bridge-building organization, not a religion.
2. We respect the sacred wisdom of each religion, spiritual expression and indigenous tradition.
3. We respect the differences among religions, spiritual expressions and indigenous traditions.
4. We encourage our members to deepen their roots in their own tradition.

5. We listen and speak with respect to deepen mutual understanding and trust.
6. We give and receive hospitality.
7. We seek and welcome the gift of diversity, and model practices that do not discriminate.
8. We practice equitable participation of women and men in all aspects of the URI.
9. We practice healing and reconciliation to resolve conflict without resorting to violence.
10. We act from sound ecological practices to protect and preserve the Earth for both present and future generations.
11. We seek and offer cooperation with other interfaith efforts.
12. We welcome as members all individuals, organizations and associations that subscribe to the Preamble, Purpose, and Principles.
13. We have the authority to make decisions at the most local level that includes all the relevant and affected parties.
14. We have the right to organize in any manner, at any scale, in any area, and around any issue or activity that is relevant to and consistent with the Preamble, Purpose, and Principles.
15. Our deliberations and decisions shall be made at every level by bodies and methods that fairly represent the diversity of affected interests and are not dominated by any.
16. We (each part of the URI) shall relinquish only such autonomy and resources as are essential to the pursuit of the Preamble, Purpose, and Principles.
17. We have the responsibility to develop financial and other resources to meet the needs of our part, and to share financial and other resources to help meet the

needs of other parts.

18. We maintain the highest standards of integrity and ethical conduct, prudent use of resources, and fair and accurate disclosure of information.

19. We are committed to organizational learning and adaptation.

20. We honor the richness and diversity of all languages and the right and responsibility of participants to translate and interpret the Charter, Articles, Bylaws and related documents in accordance with the Preamble, Purpose,and Principles, and the spirit of the United Religions Initiative.

21. Members of the URI shall not be coerced to participate in any ritual or be proselytized.

For Members of the Founder's Circle— You Are I

Now we enter the second phase of our year. In the first phase we focused, by way of early diaries, on the origins of URI...as well as the religions origins and updates on spiritual perspectives of each of the members. And circulated a compilation of interviews.

The focus for this season will be on the URI's Charter. Enclosed. It doesn't take a long time to read, maybe twenty minutes. I've written a Commentary for you on the Purpose, Preamble, and Principles to give you an idea of what we were working with at the time. This Commentary is line by line. It took me almost 20 hours to write this exercise.

What I'd like you to do is:

1. Read the complete Charter
2. With one other person or several other people read the Purpose, Preamble and Principles aloud sentence by sentence or paragraph by paragraph. It has a different power when multiple people read it aloud.
3. Read my Commentary on the Purpose, Preamble and Principles
4. Answer the questions at the end of the Commentary and send your answers to me.
5. I'll call you on the phone again and we'll chat.

Before the Charter was written:

1. In June 1996 fifty-five people decided to go for it. Create a United Religions which would be appropriately parallel to the United Nations. We called ourselves the United Religions Initiative figuring we were the scaffolding for the building of a United Religions. We knew three things: a.) it would be grassroots; b.) it would be women and men; and c.) it would have to include indigenous people. Also include people who self-described as "spiritual," e.g. Humanists, as well as people of religions.

I got two lines of credit totaling $1,000,000 and hired 4 people as the staff. They put on interfaith conferences around the world and these conferences gave us a constituency and raised excitement and potential

2. In 1997, 1998, 1999 we brought our new colleagues to Stanford University in the summertime to develop a Charter. Of course we couldn't pull it off in a conference setting but...we became a community, an international community. The Charter flowed out of this community. This kept the Charter from being an a priori head trip.

3. In 1997 we hired Dee Hock, creator of the Visa Card, to lead us in a Charter creation project. We met every six weeks for three days and this took three years. 14 people in a room with Dee. Then circulating our ideas around the world for comments and corrections. Since the genesis moment of URI came from an encounter with the United Nations, we geared this signing of our Charter with the June 26 date of the UN's Charter Signing. At the last moment we decided not to become the United Religions. We thought that title sounded ludicrous for a little group such as ours. So we figured that we would be the initiative that works toward an eventual United Religions. Thus the United Religions Initiative. By the way the lawyer who helped us wonderfully through this and the By-Laws was Peter Phleger.

A Commentary on the Preamble, Purpose and Principles

Preamble

Paragraph 1
The first words, "We, people of..." mirror the first words of the United Nations Charter. But the UN isn't about "the people." It is about the representatives of the political administrations that happen to be in power in a particular country at a particular time. We wanted to reach down below the power elites and open up global access to ordinary people of all faith persuasions. Therefore a few ordinary people have written a Charter that anticipates being an invitation to a heretofore scattered, diffuse and often powerless people of all faiths. "We, people...establish the United Religions Initiative..." The extraordinary assumption is that something is being established, something new and international. Something available to all, which will grow into a world-changing force.

Paragraph 2

When we looked around and examined the various practices of various religions, we found some things to be repugnant. So we could not say that we "affirm" each tradition and each difference. The highest word we could come up with was "respect." We can respect each other, even if some of our beliefs and practices seem odd or silly or misguided. We will never get started on building community and acting from a unified purpose if we try to appreciate and affirm every aspect of every religion. In a sense, we are taking doctrine and dogma and religious practices off the table. What we have best to confer mutually is a genuine respect for the origins, history and reality of each tradition. We respect; we don't adhere to all of the beliefs.

Paragraph 3

This is about "we," the emerging community, and about the genius of the entire Charter. If we can find enough people who are willing to "respect" people of all traditions, we can get started. URI intends to be a family of respecters. If we can gather enough people around the Charter to become a force for good in local settings, then we could collect and connect a power that would change history.

Paragraph 4

In URI we do not expect you to check your faith at the door before entering. However it is that you have been shaped by religion or spirituality; and we think this formative experience has helped to produce in you a life that aches to create community with people of other faiths. Religious divisions do not need to lead inexorably toward mutual violence. There is something generous at the core of religions, spiritual lives, and we can build on that core.

Paragraph 5

The first four paragraphs spell out URI's initial assumptions and intentions. Now we turn to eight specific targets around which we unite. We are not building up religion or spirituality or even promoting the common good. And our concern is more specific than "the common good." When you boil URI down to its essence, we exist "for the benefit of the Earth community." We are interdependent people who sense the greater interdependence and restorative health of the Earth community. Religion, itself, might well be in the service of God, but URI intends to be of service to our Earth community. We do not worship the Earth community but we, of widely different beliefs, all share a high regard for the necessity of maintaining a healthy planet Earth. United for the sake of this Earth community.

Two questions spring immediately to mind: 1) What is "the Earth community"? and 2) Are we throwing out God and replacing God with the worship of Earth or Nature...thus making us a religion of sorts - a muscular pantheism or a coy animism?

Question 1: What is "the Earth community"? We didn't define our terms, so I look back twelve years and guess at what we meant. We didn't mean earth with a small e, as in the land surface of the world. We meant capital E, the planet, third from the sun. In context of the vastness of our universe and the universes, the Earth is our island home where all living beings and plants are interdependent, and we carry the responsibility of holding up our end of the life equation along with guarding the integrity of the other life forms.

Question 2: Are we replacing God with the worship of Earth or Nature? An outside observer of URI's indigenous members carrying out their rituals at many of our meetings might assume so. A phrase such as "Divine Earth Mother" is often heard. But others words are heard as well, Allah Akbar, Jehovah, the Trinity, Higher Power, and so on. What is important to note is that we would not allow words like sacred and holy and blessed to be attached to the word "Earth." We wanted to stay away from language that elevated our planet to some Divine dimension. We placed the accent on the Earth community, not Earth Divinity. Benefiting a healthy interconnectedness of all life on this planet was goal enough for us. We didn't need to deify. Our focus was on kinship, a new model of family, in an Earth community...a big-enough tent to allow people of all the differing belief systems to find a safe meeting place.

Professor Gordon Kaufman, recently of Harvard Divinity School, argued for a vision of God as the "profound mystery of creativity," and "the ongoing creativity in the universe." He was rethinking theology in naturalistic terms...but we did not want to take one step in that direction.

Paragraph 6
We know that statements can be made and laws passed that promise an improvement in matters of justice and peace. But if the local cultures or regional cultures are not ready, the lofty words mean nothing. Furthermore in advance of changes in society, pockets of cooperation have to be in place for the seeds of change to take root. The people of URI unite to be that seedbed and to anticipate a day of greater peace and justice.

Paragraph 7
In the 1990's, when we were wrestling with this Charter, we were caught between "the tree huggers" in our group and

the cynics. What to do about environmental concern in URI's Charter and life? After years of debate we took the plunge and placed all our chips on the Earth. The healing and protection of the Earth took us out of the field of organized religions and places us squarely on the one focus where every living being or organism has a stake, to wit, the Earth. So, unashamedly, we squared the venture of URI with the venture of Earth's well-being.

Paragraph 8

One of the Charter writing group members kept saying, "URI needs to provide a safe space...where people of all faiths, contradictions, persecutions, can find a place of comfort." You can see that his language is reflected here but his thinking has been expanded. Not only solace, but also the hard work of reconciliation. If URI is to grow into relevance in a world awash with religious scar tissue, genuine grievances and unfinished business, URI must unite to address the wrongs in a manner that can bring greater healing,

Paragraph 9

Because the majority of URI members would undoubtedly come from religions, we thought that it would be important for us, straight forwardly, to take a stand on freedom of religion. But how best to do that? Since we were mostly Americans, we immediately thought of the Bill of Rights and specifically, the First Amendment to the Constitution. Yet URI is going to be made up of people from all of the countries. So, we couldn't refer to something that pertains only to one country. Our solution was to make our appeal to these rights set forth in international law.

Paragraph 10

Thinking ahead, we figured that if URI took the Earth seriously, we would inevitably be drawn into economic, environmental, political and social issues. On the one hand, URI is not intended to be primarily an advocacy group. On the other hand, there is no way to champion Earth issues without getting involved in the arenas where the fate of the Earth is determined. So, we wrote this paragraph with the understanding that entering the fray was legitimate, according to the URI Charter. Obviously, this is a delicate and potentially explosive positioning. Obviously also, we had no idea how URI would proceed—by way of Cooperation Circles, by way of Global Council positions or even how the voice of URI could be uttered in a vast, diffuse network. Nevertheless, permission needed to be given to carry out the implications of the Charter in real terms.

Paragraph 11

When we thought about big religious conferences, gatherings of prelates, or revivals, the accent was always on the great men (seldom women), the esteemed leader, or the presiding officers. That was the accepted model. What was missing was the participation in decision-making by ordinary folks, folks often in remote regions or of little status. Although we did not know how to accomplish this, URI was created to move in that direction until at last this paragraph is a reality. Meanwhile, what we wanted to do was to hold up this paragraph to our deliberations and decision-making.

Paragraph 12

This paragraph is far different in language and focus from any of the others. Why? Because we had a Buddhist at the table who was drowning in all of the official concepts and linguistic terms up till now. Here, he spoke, and was listened to. He was saying (my interpretation) that although the ordinary work of URI will be of a pragmatic nature, nevertheless in the doing of this work, and in crossing the chasms of vivid differences, we will have moments of deep and spontaneous celebration—joy and light—as we are quiet together, and as we move together. He promised us that this will come true, and that people this world over will recognize the genius of this sentiment.

Paragraph 13
Honestly I can't figure out why this paragraph is here. On a superficial level it sounds to me like some of us got carried away by the sentiments of the Buddhist and piled on with references to compassion and love. On another level, I guess it is taking into consideration that a URI will have "combined resources," and these should be invested in the wisdom of the family and in the spirit of the Charter of URI.

Purpose Statement

It took us three years to write this statement. Actually two years, eleven months, thirty days, eleven hours, and thirty minutes. Our guide, Dee Hock, instructed us that a purpose statement could only hold one thought. We spent years trying out various possibilities. Personally I came up with 10,000 (or it seemed like that number) efforts and all were rejected. When it was abundantly clear that we had three thoughts, we pulled all the strings on the corset to reduce the size, unsuccessfully. I could have lived with "and religiously-motivated violence" but others were dug in on their favorites. At this due date we had to print the Charter, of course, with the purpose. I was out of town and gave my proxy to Charles Gibbs. At the last minute we disobeyed Dee Hock and came up with a three-thought purpose.

Before you go onto this next page, would you ask yourself:
1. Which one of these could you live without?
2. What order of sequence would you have chosen?
3. Which of the three is most important?

Principles

The background for some of the principles has already been covered in the section on the Preamble, so I will not cover it again. Also I want to point out that the American Heritage Desk Dictionary says that a principle is a "basic truth, law or assumption...a rule or standard...moral or ethical standards or judgments...a fixed or predetermined policy...a basic source." In short URI people are expected to adhere to these policies. And finally some of these are self evident and need no comment from me while others are so foundational or unique that comments are called for.

Principal 1

This one has to come first. If a reader thinks that URI is a religion, all conversation is over. But if he or she understands that we are solely bridge-building between religions, then the dialogue can begin. Obviously, people bring their religions with them when they arrive at URI, so religion isn't non-mentionable. Everyone who approaches URI has to figure out what to do about his or her own faith in this interfaith setting.

Principal 2

"Respect" has been dealt with earlier. The only word of note here is the word "sacred." In writing this Charter we wrestled with terms like "Holy," "Revered," "Divine," and so on. We decided to stay as far away as possible from such words. But in this principle, we felt that "sacred" was wonderfully undefined but still reached toward the numinous dimension. Thinking subjectively, I might applaud something in a religion that I think meets the test of "sacred wisdom"—but we all don't have to agree on what that is. We respect it when we see it and we assume it is in there somewhere.

Principal 3
We don't want URI to be a Pollyanna group that pooh-poohs differences and assumes that basically we all believe the same thing. We don't. There are differences, and we are respectful of those differences.

Principal 4
We don't want people to think that they are expected to water down or abandon their faith in order to participate in URI's interfaith world. To the contrary. Living with people of other faiths tends to drive people deeper into their own faith. URI intends to be a garden; flowers rooted where they are planted, rather than a bouquet where flowers are cut off from their roots.

Principal 5
One important point here: we listen, first. Speak, second. Mutual understanding doesn't come from loquacious soliloquies but does require intense listening.

Principal 6
Working together can reap great rewards. Dialogue can move us forward. But hospitality can get to the best and most basic of traditions.

Principal 7
The more the merrier. Gifts come from unexpected sources. So in URI, discriminating against people is not an option.

Principal 8
This has the deepest roots of all in the intention of URI, and goes back to June 1996. (P.S. Our first two Chairs of the Global Council—a Jewish woman and an Indigenous woman).

Principal 9
We took this to heart immediately and started doing Conflict Resolution/Peace Building training and functioning in the Philippines, India, Uganda and Ethiopia.

Principal 10
This was the central theme that emerged from our last Global Assembly, and URI people around the world meet on a teleconference each month.

Principal 11
When we were trying to start URI, a couple of the largest interfaith organizations tried hard to sabotage us, spread untruths, and sought to get URI leaders to leave us and join them. It dawned on us that competing interfaith organizations could easily be as destructive as the competing religions they were trying to help. So from the beginning, URI would not play that game. We have a vocation to raise the level of civility and cooperation in the interfaith world.

Principal 12
Pretty straightforward. Lots of ways to be a member of URI.

Principal 13
This is crucial! It spells out that URI is a grassroots, local-level organization at heart.

Principal 14
This is crucial! The genius of URI is to be found in its self-organizing nature. It assures that URI is going to be many-faceted, and thus hard to explain.

Principal 15
There are multiple deliberations and decisions throughout

the URI system. Decisions by: Cooperation Circles, Regional Teams, Global Council, Global Staff, Assemblies, and so on. The point of this principle is that no group take it upon itself to dominate the other groups. What is prized most is having a sense of equilibrium, awareness of everyone else who is affected by one group's decisions. Peripheral vision and collaboration. This is not an invitation to talk something to death. Rather, it is about broadening the deliberation before a final decision.

Principal 16
Yes, the greatest amount of authority in URI is in the smallest unit. But is the smallest unit, while self- organizing and self-supporting in nature, in any way responsible to any other URI body? Could there ever be a situation where one part of URI is asked to relinquish some degree of authority or release some resource? Answer: Only in a special situation whereby it is essential to the pursuit of the Charter. For instance, if URI calls for a Global Assembly, it is possible to ask every CC or every Region to raise money to send their delegate.

Principal 17
On the surface, this is pretty straightforward. But tough questions lie below the surface. Should there be assessment? Who pays for a Global Assembly? A meeting of the Global Council? The other side of the coin of subsidiarity.

Principal 18
Pretty straightforward. But when it comes to having audits in seventy-eight countries of the world, the challenge appears.

Principal 19
Excellent principle. It has given us room to change and to

experiment, and to use trial and error without feeling we have offended tablets written in stone.

Here, I want to pause. Originally we had 19 principles but at the last minute—having tried them out all over the world and gotten feedback—we hurriedly added the following:

Principal 20

Ever since the first day, one problem that has dogged URI is that it might be too San Franciscan, too Christian, too white, too English in language. With effort around the world, we solved most of the concerns, speedily. All except the language part. So many people worldwide are kept away from URI simply because we have not translated our Charter into their language. This is not a secondary matter. It is primary and needs to be a principle.

Principal 21

Ritual in an interfaith setting! This is tricky. Liturgies contain enough questionable or objectionable elements to offend most anyone of another faith. Do we just gather in silence? Stay away from words? Give everyone a chance to do his or her ritual in front of others? Slice and dice liturgies with a little bit of one and a little bit of another? We are just feeling our way along, so the best we know to do is not to coerce anyone to attend any liturgy. As for proselytizing, some religious groups hurry into URI seeing it as a great venue for gaining converts. But we have to protect our people from conversion techniques. Some groups find this principle to be offensive because they want to bear witness and proselytize.

If you are still reading along, let me congratulate you on your perseverance and give you a few questions.

Questions
1. If you just read the Charter, would you imagine that URI had a chance to make a difference in the world? Why?
2. Why would religious leaders be threatened, disinterested, or excited about this Charter?
3. Do you see God in anything that is in this Charter?
4. How could money circulate through this organizational model? Why are buildings and properties never mentioned?
5. What most excited you about the Charter? What most disappoints you? Also, what else do you wish we had addressed?

I. Evolution of URI Organizational Design

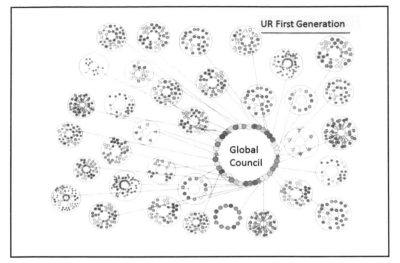

1. Hub staff is not placed in the design. Why? Because the genius of URI is that the essence is the relationship between the CC's and the GC. First, there were CC's, and these CC's created a Global Council. That's what matters. The Hub staff exists to be a resource for CC's and the Global Council and therefore in a gesture of modesty didn't need to be shown.

2. Everything else is offline: The initial charter development, the interim governance, the charter signing, the creation of funds and flow of funds, the procedure of elections, the transfer of authority, the 501 c3 status, all of the crucial details were taken for granted. And handled exclusively by the Hub staff. The quiet and unmentioned partner.

3. The Chaordic Theory of Dee Hock, while being vital to URI's birth, has normally not been successfully applied in other organizations. Why was it so successful in URI? My guess: because of the hard work of the Interim Global Council, the Hub staff and the Founder. Chaordic Theory

works if the personnel in the background keep it on track, administratively and financially. Without the quiet help keeping the Global Council and the CC network on track and moving forward, the entire enterprise would stop growing and soon fall apart.

Therefore, URI is in theory a non-bureaucratic organization, but a closer look shows that a hidden muscular bureaucracy allows the organization to flourish. This dichotomy is built into the reality of URI, even if it is absent from the original design.

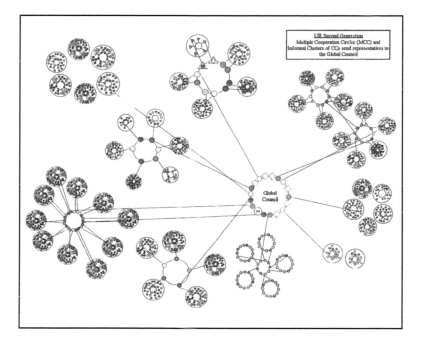

II. Observations about UR Second Generation

1) It is important to recognize that this design was not created for a URI but a UR, a second generation of UR, no less. That it, supposed we were creating a United Religions

that would parallel the United Nations, except with a diffuse structure rather than a bureaucratic structure. The hard central matter was to find a way that peoples of faith could form small, grassroots United Religions forums around the world to keep from having one large, bureaucratic forum in New York or San Francisco.

2) The crucial element in this design is that an infinite variety of formations were imagined from the beginning. Everything is intended to evolve into greater levels of complexity and possibility.

3) Notice that no thinking was imagined about Regions, Global Staff, President's Council, Joint Steering Committee, Global Assemblies. There is a core design and that is all that matters. Non-core elements are simply taken for granted. Non-core elements were expected to always show up and support the design.

4) No thought was put into imagining time commitments that would be required of volunteers. For instance, what about a person who spends time in a local CC, then spends time on an MCC, and finally is elected to spend time on the Global Council, and now has authority over the entre URI network–at no pay or reimbursement? Sort of magical thinking about volunteers who have unlimited time and no need for money.

III. Expanded Design, Part 1 – Recognize that a Hub exists

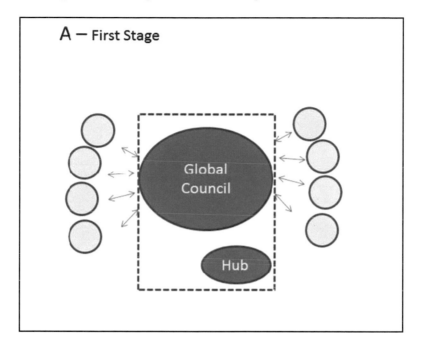

Along the way two realities had to be faced. First, Bylaws had to be written, and they had to mete out duties, responsibilities, and prerogatives of the Executive Director in the Hub office. Second, it became immediately clear that the Global Council could not keep up with all of its duties — for instance, funding the network.

Therefore, the Hub staff, which wasn't worthy of mention in the earlier designs, goes from being merely auxiliary to being, under the direction of the Executive Director, a partner in responsibilities.

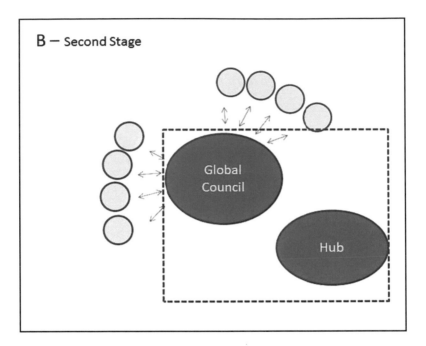

Notice that the status and influence of the Hub is rising and expanding. So, this silent partner is moving toward being an equal partner. URI finally admits what is a real situation.

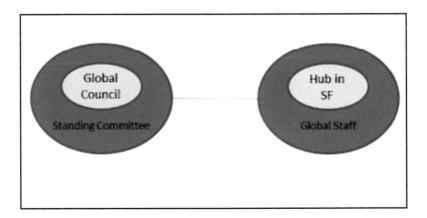

IV. Expanded Design Part 2 – Birth of Regions

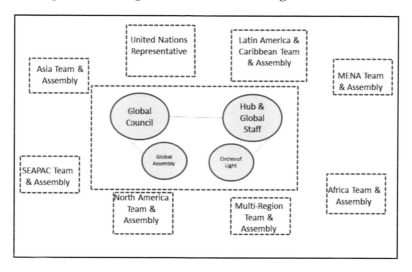

Right away it was abundantly obvious that the rapidly expanding universe of CC's could not rotate around the Hub in San Francisco. Each region would have to develop its own Hub and services for member CC's.

Borrowing from the United Nations model of seven geographic regions of the world, URI established parallel groupings of seven geographic regions.

One additional region was also established. It was non-geographic and called "multi-region." Because it is not hosted in one place but scattered everyplace, multi-region has unique challenges of community- building to go along with its impressive array of far flung and exciting CC work.

So, building on the original intent of having Regional Trustees, soon were added regional staff, regional coordinators and regional leadership teams. And in ever increasing numbers, sub-region offices.

For a multitude of reasons, but mostly financial, the plan of having a Global Assembly every three years was abandoned. Instead, most regions have their own assemblies every year. Global Assemblies remain a necessity but funding makes them difficult to hold.

Who keeps up with regional development, everyday reporting, communications, problem-solving in regions? Not the Global Council, but the Hub. By necessity, the critical work of the Hub causes it to rise in importance.

It is clear to all by now that the Hub and the Global Council have equal day-to-day importance but certainly not equal authority. Final authority for URI rests in the Global Council. Notice: Creation of a Gala, Circles of Light, which is the Hub's responsibility.

Big change also: The Hub staff expands to include regional staff members, and thus the Global Staff is created.

V. Expanded Design – Design with the President's Council

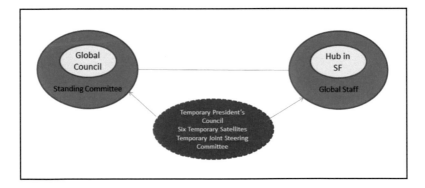

The promise and threat of a President's Council and Satellites was an unexpected structural blessing for the tiny staff at the Hub confronted with the challenges of responding to a rapidly expanding global network. It was obvious that more of everything was needed. More people walking into the office, more money, more focused expertise, more research and development, more strategic thinking. But how to obtain this more of everything?

The proposed answer: 1) create a President's Council to help the Global Council in its fundraising responsibility, and 2) create Satellites of key concerns that would attract non-Hub people to walk into the Hub offices and get to work on matters of growth, conflict resolution, leadership training, fundraising, the environment and communications. The whole strategic package was called "President's Council and Satellites."

When the package was proposed to the Global Council, there was deep concern that a President's Council might begin to usurp the authority of the Global Council and that the satellites might dominate this office or keep it from doing work.

Two solutions were forthcoming. First, the president would be granted five years to recruit a President's Council and get it up and running. At the end of the five years if the President's Council did what was intended and did not get into the arena of decision-making, it would be evaluated.

Second, the president was given permission to recruit all of the members of all of the Satellites, and to hold monthly meetings of all six. After five years, these Satellites would be evaluated as well.

In the meantime, a safeguard was built in. In order to make sure that the President's Council did not start making URI decisions, and to make sure that the Satellites did not impede the regular work of the Hub staff, a Joint Steering Committee was established to monitor progress and to determine if experiment should continue. The Joint Steering Committee was to be made up of a few members of the Global Council, the Hub staff and the President's Council. Again the Joint Steering Committee was intended to be in business five years only, 2007-2012 as a watchdog group over the President's Council

Footnote: The Senior Leadership members of the Hub eventually co-opted the five-year experiment and determined that the President's Council and the Joint Steering Committee were helpful and should remain. As for the Satellites, Senior Leadership sent a memo instructing the Satellites to be dissolved. In the end, URI ended up with two vitally important elements in its organizational design: a President's Council and a Joint Steering Committee.

VI. 2014 Expanded Design –
Evolution of the Hub/Staff Perspective

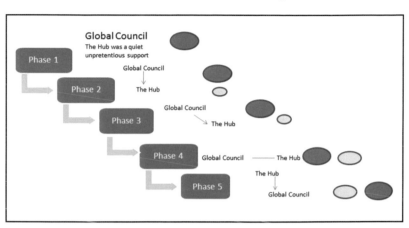

At first, URI was untouched by the Global Recession. Regular monies were coming in; URI was growing world-wide at our eighteen percent annual rate. And the Hub was stretching to keep up with the growth.

Then gradually, the financial faucet slowed, salaries were cut, institutional fatigue set in after years of unprecedented expansion and overwork, and a feeling of drifting set in at the Hub level.

URI was unable to have a Global Assembly. The Global Council of URI didn't have the money to meet for several years. When the Global Council members don't meet in person, guess who takes on more and more real authority in running of URI? The Hub. There were the years of the Hub's ascendancy, out of necessity, in power wielding.

A new Hub leadership team was assembled; ninety percent of the existing Hub staff members were replaced or released in short time; President's Council Satellites were dismantled.

What started in a Global Recession ended in a massive morale and personnel shift in the Hub. The good part was that the office became more efficient, management practices were upgraded, URI became centralized and controlled, excellent business practices were attained and linkages between the Regions and the Hub were strengthened.

But... the fear was that URI was losing its original vision of the primacy of a Global Council and Cooperation Circles, an organic and dynamic union. Instead, in an effort to be more professionally competent in its operation, URI was becoming like other standard organizations. The original silent support partner (the Hub) ends up, for the most practical purposes, becoming URI's driving force. It's worth noting in the evolution of the relationship of the Global Council and the Hub during URI organizational design 1.0- 1.9.

VII. Transition Period

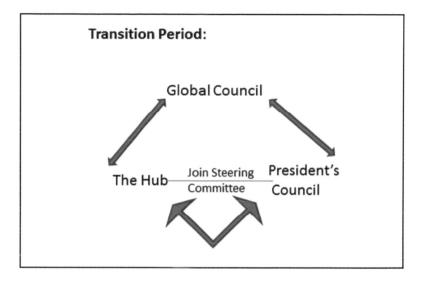

VIII. Conclusion

In the summer of 2013, both the Executive Director and the Associate Director were gone. URI 1.0 came to an end. Also, the Hub ceased to be led by Executives, and then became a collaborative team functioning in a leadership posture, but more in a position of assisting the URI network.

The body that stepped forward to deliberate and make final recommendations to the Global Council was the Joint Steering Committee, which is made up of members of the Global Council, the Global Staff and the President's Council. The Joint Steering Committee had evolved from being a temporary watchdog group to being the reliable seat of critical deliberations. With the three central authorities working together in an equitable way, the organizational design of URI had matured under the pressures of necessity to the point that all three parties were in place and eager to work together and get on with URI 2.0.

Proposals for a United Religions: 1893—1996

A Brief and Incomplete History
As listed in *The Coming United Religions* by William E. Swing, 1998

This information comes primarily from a paper presented by the Rev. Marcus Braybrooke in April 1996 at Westminster College, Oxford, at an International Interfaith Centre Conference.

1893: The World's Parliament of Religions: The idea of a united religions came, along with many other proposals.

Early 1920s: Rudolph Otto suggested the creation of an Inter-Religious League, as a parallel to the League of Nations.

1930s: In his Book, *The Religious Foundation of Internationalism*, Dr. Norman Bentwich called for a League of Religions, and said the idea had a long history including such proponents as Leibnitz and Rousseau.

World Congress of Faiths was founded in the 1930s by Sir Francis Younghusband, who wrote that, "a religious basis is essential for the new world order."

1943: Dr. George Bell, Bishop of Chichester, facilitated the establishment of an interfaith committee to provide, "an association between International Authority and representatives of the living religions of the world," and produced the Three Faith Declaration (Protestant, Catholic, Jewish) to be presented to the UN, but was largely ignored.

1950s on: Starting with Secretary General U Thant in the 1940s, every decade has heard a U.N. proposal for something like the United Religions.

1950s: World Alliance of Religions held some conferences.

1952: World Parliament of Religions was founded at Presbyterian Labor Temple in New York to establish a permanent group, "to work with a permanent United Nations to stop the war and the causes of war and to extend the more abundant life among all peoples on earth."

1960s-1990s: The Temple of Understanding held Spiritual Summit Conferences to parallel Summit Conferences of world leaders.

1961-1996: Won Buddhists of Korea: Prime Masters of Won Buddhism have presented an idea of a united religions to lead in solving the spiritual problems of the world.

1970s: Sri R.R. Diwaker, one of the founders of the World Conference on Religion and Peace, expressed the need for a "united religious organization of the whole world."

1986: A World Council of Faiths was suggested by Dr. John Taylor at a meeting of large international interfaith organizations at Ammerdown, England, but failed to gain support.

1993: At the Chicago Parliament of the World's Religions, the idea was proposed by Sir Sigmund Sternberg, Chair of International Council of Christians and Jews, and by Dr. Robert Muller, former Assistant Secretary General of the United Nations, and was endorsed by many others. The

Council for a Parliament of the World's Religions later explored whether it could pursue the vision, but concluded that a united religions organization was beyond its grasp.

1995: Although its vision was not a united religions organization, the Peace Council was formed as an organization of internationally known individuals to work together and support each other's work for global peacemaking.

1996: The San Francisco Summit Meeting for a Global United Religions Initiative approved the proposal of a united religions that would begin with the purpose of pursuing peace among religions for the sake of the entire order of life. This United Religions had a target date of the year 2000 for its charter signing.

Tribute to Charles Gibbs
June 2014

My reflection is entitled: The five most important words in the history of URI.

Starting in 1993, I began preaching, talking, bluffing, exhorting, prattling on all over the world about the coming United Religions. Stirring the religious communities as hard as I could. Sparks flew and in my wake was considerable chaos. The Spirit hovered over that watery mist until, at last, order began to spring forth from the chaos. Three pillars emerged that proved to be foundation upon which the United Religions Initiative would forever rest.

The first pillar was the Hub in San Francisco. Although we have always shied away from admitting and stating the obvious for fear of looking power hungry, the Hub was and is nonetheless the primary unit of URI. Everything that URI has become ushered forth from the first Hub, from four people in an office in 1996. They planned our original URI conferences, fashioned our first budget, obtained the 50lc3 status, carried out the Stanford summer conferences, set in place the rudimentary bodies of governance, and recruited from all over the world. That legacy goes on to this very day. The Hub manages the URI world, and the person in charge of the Hub is the most important person in URI.

Charles Gibbs sat in the seat of authority in the Hub for the first fourteen years of URI's coming to maturity. Obviously the trick has been to move authority and power away from the Hub to the CC's and Regions; nevertheless, the day to day power and authority is the Hub's to give away or monopolize. Part of Charles's greatness is that he did not clutch at his prerogative but actually kept the power flowing and circulating. Charles is by nature a courtly and a gentle man. His style is not to accumulate power but to circulate power. The precedence that he established , the model of servant leader, is now the expected model for the person in charge of the Hub.

The second pillar was The Community of URI. Clearly, I speak about the summer gatherings at Stanford University, where people from all over the world came to write a Charter... and failed miserably. But a greater thing happened... they fell in love with each other and sensed the vast potential for peace-building that burned in their midst.

Charles made no memorable speeches on those occasions. He did something far more important. He got to know and cherish each and every person who showed up. Yes, we ended up with lots of individual stories and information on computers, but far more important, Charles carried those stories and information in his heart. That is why so many people felt empowered to create URI.

The third pillar was the Charter. In my un-humble opinion the URI Charter is the most important interfaith document of the first part of the twenty-first century. In the three years it took to write the Charter, Charles was the most diligent, thoughtful, passionate, careful person at the table. And why shouldn't he have been? That Charter was created to be a mirror of Charles's intuition and spiritual instincts. His DNA is awash in the Charter's words.

So, I look back at the three pillars upon which URI rests, and upon the unmistakable impression that Charles has made on the origin and destiny of URI, and I ask myself...what are the five most important words in our history? Answer: When the Rev. Charles Gibbs came up to me in the mid 1 990's and said, "I would like to help." The rest is history. Thank you, Charles, for your offer.

Peace Comes Piecemeal

Blog Post on URI.com
December 13, 2012
By William E. Swing

One of our President's Council members, George by name, stopped in the doorway following a meeting and announced, "I finally got it. Peace is made by multiple small actions happening at the same time. Peace isn't one big thing; it is lots of little things happening in concert...youth, women, conflict resolution, marches, medicines, dialogues, and so on. Peace comes piecemeal." That is exactly how URI sees it and does it.

Take today, December 13, 2012. I scan my email and here's what I see. Five new Cooperation Circles. In Malawi: Muslim, Pentecostal, Seventh Day Adventist and Presbyterian youth training in self-reliant citizenship. In India: working with poor people who are dealing with AIDS, TB and cancer. In Chile: Mapuche indigenous people coming together to heal the Earth. In Israel: teaching modern Arabic to Jewish students and adults to help them appreciate Muslim culture. In Alexandria, Egypt: creating a Youth Media Channel to assist human rights, gender equality and freedom of expression. All small pieces of a large goal of peace.

Today I check out the second report from India written by URI's Executive Director, Charles Gibbs. He speaks of a

Swami who wants to fund a meeting space, room and board for 250 people for next year's URI India meeting. He speaks of the Nobel Prize winning Rabindranath Tagore, whose life was turned around by his father's vision of various religions, when his father stood by a tree where people worshiped God as One. Then there was a Cooperation Circle with over 5,000 musicians, a CC that is cross-caste as well as inter-religious. And finally, in February, in the midst of a mass Hindu Pilgrimage, Kumbh Mela, where 130 million people are expected to participate in ritual bathing and discussions of religious doctrine, a URI CC is hosting the first ever Green Interfaith Kumbh Mela, which is dedicated to cleaning the Ganges, as part of the larger gathering. Small daily, enduring pieces of peace.

In the news this day are Syria, Palestine, Jerusalem and Uganda. I know that today, one of URI's Cooperation Circles in Jordan is distributing clothes, household appliances, blankets and children's toys to refugees from Syria. Today in Pakistan, our URI youth are traveling 80 miles through Taliban strongholds to witness to peace along the Afghan/Iran border. Also in Pakistan, 500 students from the Agricultural University in Rawalpindi, students who are beset by "bias, phobias and fear," are being introduced to URI's Charter and programs in a great assembly. In Jerusalem, our Peacemakers CC has just celebrated "Jerusalem, A Capital of Peace" (Certainly a revolutionary idea at this moment). And in Northern Uganda, where 12,000 lands cases need to be adjudicated, one of our CCs is launching mediation sessions in the districts of Lamwo, Gulu, Kitgum, Amuru and Nwoya. If "peace" were plural, it would be "peaces."

What is URI like? It is like standing up very close to an impressionistic painting. Up close it looks like dabs and blotches and odd configurations. But when you step back, what comes into view might by a beautiful stream or a bridge or flowers. That is what URI is like. To witness one or two colorful strokes of URI hardly paints the picture. But when the entire landscape comes into perspective, a potential masterpiece is being created. Pieces can make a master peace. Or as George said, "Peace comes piecemeal."

PRESIDENT'S COUNCIL PRAYER
the Rt. Rev. William E. Swing

We make our prayer to the One who is worthy of praise
    at the beginning of time and the end of time,
    to the One whose presence today is Glory in our midst;

In the disease of religious violence inspire us to anticipate
    the cure of peace among believers of all traditions;

In the face of spiritual arrogance that falsely elevates one
believer over others
    and sows the seeds of mistaken superiority

Help us to stand in humility before Your throne; and

In the face of the accepted creed that religious rivalries are
inevitable
    and impenetrable, make us slaves
    to the extravagant hope that wholeness is possible.

At this critical time of religious brokenness and rising threat,
challenge us
    to be stewards of that sacred equilibrium which is at
    the heart of harmonies and families and communities.

We beg your blessing that our work as a Council may
    be effective in the world and honorable in Your sight.

    Amen